OPPOSING VIEWPOINTS® SERIES

The Middle East

Other Books of Related Interest:

Opposing Viewpoints Series

Iraq

At Issue Series

How Should the U.S. Proceed in Afghanistan?

Current Controversies Series

Darfur

"Congress shall make no law . . . abridging the freedom of speech, or of the press."

First Amendment to the U.S. Constitution

The basic foundation of our democracy is the First Amendment guarantee of freedom of expression. The Opposing Viewpoints Series is dedicated to the concept of this basic freedom and the idea that it is more important to practice it than to enshrine it.

OPPOSING
VIEWPOINTS®
SERIES

The Middle East

*David M. Haugen, Susan Musser and Kacy Lovelace,
Book Editors*

GREENHAVEN PRESS
A part of Gale, Cengage Learning

GALE
CENGAGE Learning™

Detroit • New York • San Francisco • New Haven, Conn • Waterville, Maine • London

Christine Nasso, *Publisher*
Elizabeth Des Chenes, *Managing Editor*

© 2009 Greenhaven Press, a part of Gale, Cengage Learning.

Gale and Greenhaven Press are registered trademarks used herein under license.

For more information, contact:
Greenhaven Press
27500 Drake Rd.
Farmington Hills, MI 48331-3535
Or you can visit our Internet site at gale.cengage.com

For product information and technology assistance, contact us at

Gale Customer Support, 1-800-877-4253
For permission to use material from this text or product, submit all requests online at www.cengage.com/permissions

Further permissions questions can be emailed to permissionrequest@cengage.com

Articles in Greenhaven Press anthologies are often edited for length to meet page requirements. In addition, original titles of these works are changed to clearly present the main thesis and to explicitly indicate the author's opinion. Every effort is made to ensure that Greenhaven Press accurately reflects the original intent of the authors. Every effort has been made to trace the owners of copyrighted material.

Cover photograph reproduced by permission of Olivier Laban-Mattei/AFP/Getty Images.

LIBRARY OF CONGRESS CATALOGING-IN-PUBLICATION DATA

The Middle East / David M. Haugen, Susan Musser, and Kacy Lovelace, book editors.
   p. cm. -- (Opposing viewpoints)
Includes bibliographical references and index.
ISBN 978-0-7377-4532-0 (hardcover)
ISBN 978-0-7377-4533-7 (pbk.)
1. United States--Foreign relations--Middle East. 2. Middle East--Foreign relations--United States. 3. United States--Foreign relations--Middle East--Sources. 4. Middle East--Foreign relations--United States--Sources. I. Haugen, David M., 1969- II. Musser, Susan. III. Lovelace, Kacy.
DS63.2.U5M425 2009
327.73056--dc22
                                              2008055848

Printed in the United States of America
1 2 3 4 5 6 7 13 12 11 10 09

Contents

Chapter 3: Is Iran a Threat to the United States and Its Allies?

Chapter 4: How Are Middle Eastern Nations Addressing the War on Terrorism?

Why Consider Opposing Viewpoints?

"The only way in which a human being can make some approach to knowing the whole of a subject is by hearing what can be said about it by persons of every variety of opinion and studying all modes in which it can be looked at by every character of mind. No wise man ever acquired his wisdom in any mode but this."

John Stuart Mill

In our media-intensive culture it is not difficult to find differing opinions. Thousands of newspapers and magazines and dozens of radio and television talk shows resound with differing points of view. The difficulty lies in deciding which opinion to agree with and which "experts" seem the most credible. The more inundated we become with differing opinions and claims, the more essential it is to hone critical reading and thinking skills to evaluate these ideas. Opposing Viewpoints books address this problem directly by presenting stimulating debates that can be used to enhance and teach these skills. The varied opinions contained in each book examine many different aspects of a single issue. While examining these conveniently edited opposing views, readers can develop critical thinking skills such as the ability to compare and contrast authors' credibility, facts, argumentation styles, use of persuasive techniques, and other stylistic tools. In short, the Opposing Viewpoints Series is an ideal way to attain the higher-level thinking and reading skills so essential in a culture of diverse and contradictory opinions.

In addition to providing a tool for critical thinking, Opposing Viewpoints books challenge readers to question their own strongly held opinions and assumptions. Most people form their opinions on the basis of upbringing, peer pressure, and personal, cultural, or professional bias. By reading carefully balanced opposing views, readers must directly confront new ideas as well as the opinions of those with whom they disagree. This is not to simplistically argue that everyone who reads opposing views will—or should—change his or her opinion. Instead, the series enhances readers' understanding of their own views by encouraging confrontation with opposing ideas. Careful examination of others' views can lead to the readers' understanding of the logical inconsistencies in their own opinions, perspective on why they hold an opinion, and the consideration of the possibility that their opinion requires further evaluation.

Evaluating Other Opinions

To ensure that this type of examination occurs, Opposing Viewpoints books present all types of opinions. Prominent spokespeople on different sides of each issue as well as well-known professionals from many disciplines challenge the reader. An additional goal of the series is to provide a forum for other, less known, or even unpopular viewpoints. The opinion of an ordinary person who has had to make the decision to cut off life support from a terminally ill relative, for example, may be just as valuable and provide just as much insight as a medical ethicist's professional opinion. The editors have two additional purposes in including these less known views. One, the editors encourage readers to respect others' opinions—even when not enhanced by professional credibility. It is only by reading or listening to and objectively evaluating others' ideas that one can determine whether they are worthy of consideration. Two, the inclusion of such viewpoints encourages the important critical thinking skill of objectively evaluating an author's credentials and bias. This evaluation will illuminate an author's reasons for taking a particular stance on an issue and will aid in readers' evaluation of the author's ideas.

It is our hope that these books will give readers a deeper understanding of the issues debated and an appreciation of the complexity of even seemingly simple issues when good and honest people disagree. This awareness is particularly important in a democratic society such as ours in which people enter into public debate to determine the common good. Those with whom one disagrees should not be regarded as enemies but rather as people whose views deserve careful examination and may shed light on one's own.

Thomas Jefferson once said that "difference of opinion leads to inquiry, and inquiry to truth." Jefferson, a broadly educated man, argued that "if a nation expects to be ignorant and free . . . it expects what never was and never will be." As individuals and as a nation, it is imperative that we consider the opinions of others and examine them with skill and discernment. The Opposing Viewpoints Series is intended to help readers achieve this goal.

David L. Bender and Bruno Leone,
Founders

Introduction

> *"We must declare war on poverty and take serious measures to eradicate it. This entails fighting corruption, waste and various forms of pollution, not only of nature, but also of societal values. The current surge in oil and gas prices must be put to good use to avoid a repeat performance of what happened with the first oil price hike."*
>
> Mohamed Sid-Ahmed,
> Al-Ahram, October 24, 2005.

> *"To win the war on terror, we must first stop enabling terrorism with our oil money. Let's instead use our money to fund a war on oil. Corn ethanol has served us well and has paved the way for our future energy security. It has shown America that we do have alternatives to oil."*
>
> Vinod Khosla,
> Wall Street Journal, January 23, 2007.

The 1970s and 1980s witnessed the end of a great boon for many Middle Eastern economies because of the rising demand for oil, the region's greatest money-making resource. But instead of reinvesting oil profits into building local economies and improving roads and other aspects of national infrastructure, those leaders who benefited from oil wealth tended to lock their money up in foreign bank accounts or invest it in foreign markets. The result was that in 1986 when the oil market collapsed and prices fell from $40 to $12 a barrel,

Middle Eastern oil producers began depleting their reserves to fend off disaster. But it was only a delaying tactic. By the 1990s, many nations such as Kuwait and Saudi Arabia were forced to borrow money from international lenders. Without a diversified economy to buffer the problem, these countries' domestic debt rose precipitously.

In the months after al Qaeda terrorists crashed hijacked airliners into targets on U.S. soil in September 2001, pundits across the globe began linking increased poverty in Middle Eastern nations with the rise of militant extremism. Indeed, the White House pledged to boost foreign aid to poor countries, in part, to counteract this supposed trend. In March 2002 President George W. Bush affirmed, "We fight against poverty because hope is an answer to terror." While several scholars have denied that there is a correlation between poverty and terrorism, the popular conception remains. In a 2008 article for the *International Herald Tribune*, Kenneth M. Pollack, a senior fellow at the Brookings Institution's Saban Center for Middle East Policy, suggested that the new oil boon of the twenty-first century gives Middle Eastern countries a chance to address "the deep-seated political, economic and social problems that have spawned terrorist groups like al Qaeda."

Pollack claims that a few Mideast countries are trying to avoid past pitfalls. "This time around," he writes, "some Middle Eastern oil producers are trying to be smarter. They are investing billions of dollars at home, building industries, repairing roads and factories, and expanding social services." But Pollack contends that the spending is on big projects designed to reap quick profits; many of the Arab governments are ignoring small scale economic incentives and thus have done little to reduce poverty and unemployment. He credits only King Abdullah of Saudi Arabia with promoting "the kind of meaningful investment that, over time, could lift the Saudi labor force out of its dangerous doldrums."

While some hope that redressing poverty in Arab nations with petrodollars will counteract terrorism, others see a connection between oil wealth and extremism. The Institute for the Analysis of Global Security, a nonprofit educational organization, argues that oil profits in countries like Saudi Arabia are commonly funneled into false charities that feed terrorist groups. The Institute asserts that "it is no coincidence that so much of the cash filling terrorists' coffers comes from the oil monarchies in the Persian Gulf. It is also no coincidence that those countries holding the world's largest oil reserves and those generating most of their income from oil exports, are also those with the strongest support for radical Islam." On its Web site, the Institute quotes under secretary of the treasury Stuart Levey in a 2005 statement before Congress as saying, "Wealthy Saudi financiers and charities have funded terrorist organizations and causes that support terrorism and the ideology that fuels the terrorists' agenda. Even today, we believe that Saudi donors may still be a significant source of terrorist financing, including for the insurgency in Iraq."

Unlike Pollack, the Institute for the Analysis of Global Security has little faith that oil producers will take any steps to address this problem. The Institute maintains that the Saudi government, for example, "has been complicit in its people's actions and has turned a blind eye" to oil financiers sending money to terrorists. The Institute supports the view that only America and other committed nations can cripple the flow of funds by investing in alternative energies and decreasing dependence on Middle Eastern oil.

Although few Arab oil producers are eager to see their best customers switch to biofuels and clean energy technologies, they are willing to enlist in the U.S.-led war on terrorism. Even if, for example, Saudi Arabia is turning a blind eye to its citizens' financing of terrorism or failing to make meaningful investments that might break any connections between poverty and extremism, the Saudi regime has allied itself with the

United States in stamping out terrorist threats. Many other Middle East oil nations—such as Bahrain, Kuwait, Syria, and the United Arab Emirates—have also pledged their support for the war on terror despite accusations of funding or tolerating terrorists in their midst.

Some of these governments may have taken this anti-terror stance because of improved relations with and aid from the United States. According to Andrew C. McCarthy, a senior fellow at the Foundation for the Defense of Democracies, the United Arab Emirates turned vigilant in its anti-terror stance in hopes of continuing to receive U.S. arms shipments to fend off aggressive neighbors like Iran. Other Mideast governments, however, are aware that terrorists tend to be an unpredictable and destabilizing force in their home countries. The Saudi monarchy began its crackdown on extremism in 2003 after terrorists carried out several bombings within the kingdom. Many such countries, in which the oil wealth is not trickling down to the poor masses, are beefing up counterterrorism efforts in order to quell possible revolution from the mosques and religious schools where extremist ideology is nurtured.

How the Middle East will juggle oil and terrorism will prove how stable the region and its players will be during the protracted war on terror. Diversification and development as well as stricter laws against extremism may put terrorism to rest. On the other hand, high oil prices could bring greater U.S. involvement in the region as well as more capital for terrorist causes. And, of course, oil is just one factor affecting the search for security in the Middle East and the world at large.

In *Opposing Viewpoints: The Middle East*, various authors examine oil, terrorism, and some of the other aspects of the region that are improving or impeding stability. In chapters entitled How Should the United States Address Problems in the Middle East? How Can There Be Peace Between Israel and Palestine? Is Iran a Threat to the United States and Its Allies? and How Are Middle Eastern Nations Addressing the War on

Terrorism? critics and commentators from the Middle East and America debate the impact of internal and external forces on keeping peace in one of the more volatile regions on the globe.

OPPOSING
VIEWPOINTS®
SERIES

CHAPTER 1

How Should the United States Address Problems in the Middle East?

Chapter Preface

On January 13, 2008, United States President George W. Bush gave a speech discussing freedom in the Middle East in Abu Dhabi, United Arab Emirates. The president used this opportunity to reiterate the United States' commitment to pursuing peace in the Middle East, and promoting freedom in the volatile region. And in doing so, he pointed out the various agents of instability that posed a threat to peace in the Middle East.

The president identified Iran's support of terrorist regimes as a main cause of insecurity in the Middle East. According to President Bush, Tehran's funding of terrorist groups such as Hezbollah, Hamas, and the Palestinian Islamic Jihad has allowed Iran to further its own ambitions for power in the Middle East while hindering peacekeeping in the region. Additionally, he blamed Iran's leaders for supplying both the Shiite militants in Iraq and the Taliban resistance in Afghanistan with weapons to carry out their agenda of terror.

President Bush also highlighted the continuing threat from the terrorist group al Qaeda, the organization behind the September 11, 2001, attacks on the United States. He claimed that al Qaeda was responsible for numerous deaths of U.S. and coalition troops as well as innocent civilians in Afghanistan and Iraq. Bush told the assembled Arab dignitaries that al Qaeda's goal is to, "topple your governments, acquire weapons of mass destruction, and drive a wedge between the people of the United States and the people of the Middle East."

In his speech, Bush assured his audience that the United States will aid the countries of the Middle East in their effort to vanquish the causes of instability and to "build the institutions of democracy and prosperity." He also promised to help defeat "common enemies," launch programs that provide education and economic reform, promote peace negotiations, and protect the people and borders of every country with which the United States forges alliances. President Bush closed by addressing the people of the Middle East, asserting that America "hears your cries for justice. We share your desire for a free and prosperous future. And as you struggle to find your voice and make your way in this world, the United States will stand with you."

In the following chapter, various authors discuss U.S. involvement in the Middle East and its impact on the region. Some support America's increased commitment to Arab nations, while others fear that too much U.S. involvement can aggravate the forces of instability and ultimately cause more harm than good.

| *"Once people even get a small taste of liberty, they're not going to rest until they're free."*

The United States Should Promote Democracy in the Middle East

George W. Bush

President George W. Bush argues in the following viewpoint that the United States must promote democracy in the Middle East because it is essential to stabilizing that region and increasing American national security. He invokes the creation of a democratic Japan following World War II as an analogy to what will happen in the Middle East and Iraq if the United States is vigilant and steadfast in its efforts to create democratic governments there. George W. Bush is the forty-third President of the United States and presided over the U.S. invasion of Iraq in 2003.

As you read, consider the following questions:

1. According to the author, what reasons did critics give to support their claim that a democratic government would never work in Japan?

George W. Bush, "President Bush Attends Veterans of Foreign Wars National Convention, Discusses War on Terror," whitehouse.gov, August 22, 2007.

2. What does Bush cite to be evidence of the strong desire in the Middle East for democratic reform?

3. Bush states that a free Iraq will be different than the Iraq that existed under Saddam Hussein in what ways?

I [am] a wartime President. I wish I didn't have to say that, but an enemy that attacked us on September the 11th, 2001, declared war on the United States of America. And war is what we're engaged in. The struggle has been called a clash of civilizations. In truth, it's a struggle for civilization. We fight for a free way of life against a new barbarism—an ideology whose followers have killed thousands on American soil, and seek to kill again on even a greater scale.

We fight for the possibility that decent men and women across the broader Middle East can realize their destiny—and raise up societies based on freedom and justice and personal dignity. And as long as I'm commander-in-chief we will fight to win. I'm confident that we will prevail. I'm confident we'll prevail because we have the greatest force for human liberation the world has ever known—the men and women of the United States Armed Forces. . . .

Attacks on Freedom

I want to open . . . with a story that begins on a sunny morning, when thousands of Americans were murdered in a surprise attack—and our nation was propelled into a conflict that would take us to every corner of the globe.

The enemy who attacked us despises freedom, and harbors resentment at the slights he believes America and Western nations have inflicted on his people. He fights to establish his rule over an entire region. And over time, he turns to a strategy of suicide attacks destined to create so much carnage that the American people will tire of the violence and give up the fight.

If this story sounds familiar, it is—except for one thing. The enemy I have just described is not al Qaeda, and the attack is not 9/11, and the empire is not the radical caliphate envisioned by Osama bin Laden. Instead, what I've described is the war machine of Imperial Japan in the 1940s, its surprise attack on Pearl Harbor, and its attempt to impose its empire throughout East Asia.

Ultimately, the United States prevailed in World War II, and we have fought two more land wars in Asia. . . . Yet even the most optimistic . . . probably would not have foreseen that the Japanese would transform themselves into one of America's strongest and most steadfast allies, or that the South Koreans would recover from enemy invasion to raise up one of the world's most powerful economies, or that Asia would pull itself out of poverty and hopelessness as it embraced markets and freedom.

The lesson from Asia's development is that the heart's desire for liberty will not be denied. Once people even get a small taste of liberty, they're not going to rest until they're free. Today's dynamic and hopeful Asia—a region that brings us countless benefits—would not have been possible without America's presence and perseverance. . . .

Winning Ideological Struggles

There are many differences between the wars we fought in the Far East and the war on terror we're fighting today. But one important similarity is at their core they're ideological struggles. The militarists of Japan and the Communists in Korea and Vietnam were driven by a merciless vision for the proper ordering of humanity. They killed Americans because we stood in the way of their attempt to force their ideology on others. Today, the names and places have changed, but the fundamental character of the struggle has not changed. Like our enemies in the past, the terrorists who wage war in Iraq and Afghanistan and other places seek to spread a political vision of their own—a harsh plan for life that crushes freedom, tolerance, and dissent.

Like our enemies in the past, they kill Americans because we stand in their way of imposing this ideology across a vital region of the world. This enemy is dangerous; this enemy is determined; and this enemy will be defeated.

We're still in the early hours of the current ideological struggle, but we do know how the others ended—and that knowledge helps guide our efforts today. The ideals and interests that led America to help the Japanese turn defeat into democracy are the same that lead us to remain engaged in Afghanistan and Iraq.

The defense strategy that refused to hand the South Koreans over to a totalitarian neighbor helped raise up [an] Asian Tiger that is the model for developing countries across the world, including the Middle East. The result of American sacrifice and perseverance in Asia is a freer, more prosperous and stable continent whose people want to live in peace with America, not attack America.

At the outset of World War II there were only two democracies in the Far East—Australia and New Zealand. Today most of the nations in Asia are free, and its democracies reflect the diversity of the region. Some of these nations have constitutional monarchies, some have parliaments, and some have presidents. Some are Christian, some are Muslim, some are Hindu, and some are Buddhist. Yet for all the differences, the free nations of Asia all share one thing in common: Their governments derive their authority from the consent of the governed, and they desire to live in peace with their neighbors.

Along the way to this freer and more hopeful Asia, there were a lot of doubters. Many times in the decades that followed World War II, American policy in Asia was dismissed as hopeless and naive. And when we listen to criticism of the difficult work our generation is undertaking in the Middle East today, we can hear the echoes of the same arguments made about the Far East years ago.

They Said a Democracy Wouldn't Work in Japan

In the aftermath of Japan's surrender, many thought it naive to help the Japanese transform themselves into a democracy. Then as now, the critics argued that some people were simply not fit for freedom.

Some said Japanese culture was inherently incompatible with democracy. Joseph Grew, a former United States ambassador to Japan who served as Harry Truman's under secretary of state, told the President flatly that—and I quote—"democracy in Japan would never work." He wasn't alone in that belief. A lot of Americans believed that—and so did the Japanese—a lot of Japanese believed the same thing: democracy simply wouldn't work.

Other critics said that Americans were imposing their ideals on the Japanese. For example, Japan's Vice Prime Minister asserted that allowing Japanese women to vote would "retard the progress of Japanese politics."

It's interesting what [World War II] General [Douglas] MacArthur wrote in his memoirs. He wrote, "There was much criticism of my support for the enfranchisement of women. Many Americans, as well as many other so-called experts, expressed the view that Japanese women were too steeped in the tradition of subservience to their husbands to act with any degree of political independence." That's what General MacArthur observed. In the end, Japanese women were given the vote; 39 women won parliamentary seats in Japan's first free election. Today, Japan's minister of defense is a woman, and just last month [July 2007], a record number of women were elected to Japan's Upper House.

There are other critics, believe it or not, that argue that democracy could not succeed in Japan because the national religion—Shinto—was too fanatical and rooted in the Emperor. Senator Richard Russell denounced the Japanese faith, and said that if we did not put the Emperor on trial, "any steps we may take to create democracy are doomed to failure." The State Department's man in Tokyo put it bluntly: "The Emperor system must disappear if Japan is ever really to be democratic."

One of America's Strongest Allies

Those who said Shinto was incompatible with democracy were mistaken, and fortunately, Americans and Japanese leaders recognized it at the time, because instead of suppressing the Shinto faith, American authorities worked with the Japanese to institute religious freedom for all faiths. Instead of abolishing the imperial throne, Americans and Japanese worked together to find a place for the Emperor in the democratic political system.

And the result of all these steps was that every Japanese citizen gained freedom of religion, and the Emperor remained on his throne and Japanese democracy grew stronger because it embraced a cherished part of Japanese culture. And today, in defiance of the critics and the doubters and the skeptics, Japan retains its religions and cultural traditions, and stands as one of the world's great free societies.

You know, the experts sometimes get it wrong. An interesting observation, one historian [MIT professor John Dower] put it—he said, "Had these erstwhile experts"—he was talking about people criticizing the efforts to help Japan realize the blessings of a free society—he said, "Had these erstwhile experts had their way, the very notion of inducing a democratic revolution would have died of ridicule at an early stage."

Instead, I think it's important to look at what happened. A democratic Japan has brought peace and prosperity to its people. Its foreign trade and investment have helped jumpstart the economies of others in the region. The alliance between our two nations is the lynchpin for freedom and stability throughout the Pacific. And I want you to listen carefully to this final point: Japan has transformed from America's en-

The Battle of Ideas

The war on terror is, after all, more than a contest of arms and more than a test of will. It is also a battle of ideas. To prevail in the long run, we have to remove the conditions that inspire such blind, prideful hatred that drove 19 men to get onto airliners to come kill us [in the terror attacks on September 11, 2001]. Many have noted that we're in a struggle for the "hearts and minds" of people in a troubled region of the world. That is true and it should give us confidence. Outside a small and cruel circle, it's hard to imagine anybody being won over, intellectually or emotionally, by random violence, the beheading of bound men, children's television programs that exalt suicide bombing, and the desecration of mosques. The extremists in the Middle East are not really trying to win hearts and minds, but to paralyze them, to seize power by force, to keep power by intimidation, and to build an empire of fear.

We offer a nobler alternative. We know from history that when people live in freedom, have their rights respected and have real hope for the future, they will not be drawn in by ideologies that stir up hatreds and incite violence. We know, as well, that when men and women are given the chance, most by far will choose to live in freedom. That's the cause we serve today in Afghanistan and Iraq—helping the peoples of those two nations to achieve security, peace, and the right to chart their own destiny. . . . We are helping them fight back because it's the right thing to do, and because the outcome is important to our own long-term security.

Dick Cheney,
Vice President's Remarks to the Washington
Institute for Near East Policy, October 21, 2007.

emy in the ideological struggle of the 20th century to one of America's strongest allies in the ideological struggle of the 21st century. . . .

The Lessons of History

I recognize that history cannot predict the future with absolute certainty. I understand that. But history does remind us that there are lessons applicable to our time. And we can learn something from history. In Asia, we saw freedom triumph over violent ideologies after the sacrifice of tens of thousands of American lives—and that freedom has yielded peace for generations.

The American military graveyards across Europe attest to the terrible human cost in the fight against Nazism. They also attest to the triumph of a continent that today is whole, free, and at peace. The advance of freedom in these lands should give us confidence that the hard work we are doing in the Middle East can have the same results we've seen in Asia and elsewhere—if we show the same perseverance and the same sense of purpose.

In a world where the terrorists are willing to act on their twisted beliefs with sickening acts of barbarism, we must put faith in the timeless truths about human nature that have made us free.

Across the Middle East, millions of ordinary citizens are tired of war, they're tired of dictatorship and corruption, they're tired of despair. They want societies where they're treated with dignity and respect, where their children have the hope for a better life. They want nations where their faiths are honored and they can worship in freedom.

And that is why millions of Iraqis and Afghans turned out to the polls—millions turned out to the polls. And that's why their leaders have stepped forward at the risk of assassination. And that's why tens of thousands are joining the security forces of their nations. These men and women are taking great risks to build a free and peaceful Middle East—and for the sake of our own security, we must not abandon them.

Fighting the War for Democracy

There is one group of people who understand the stakes, understand as well as any expert, anybody in America—those are the men and women in uniform. Through nearly six years of war, they have performed magnificently. Day after day, hour after hour, they keep the pressure on the enemy that would do our citizens harm. They've overthrown two of the most brutal tyrannies of the world, and liberated more than 50 million citizens.

In Iraq, our troops are taking the fight to the extremists and radicals and murderers all throughout the country. Our troops have killed or captured an average of more than 1,500 al Qaeda terrorists and other extremists every month since January of this year [2007]. We're in the fight. Today our troops are carrying out a surge that is helping bring former Sunni insurgents into the fight against the extremists and radicals, into the fight against al Qaeda, into the fight against the enemy that would do us harm. They're clearing out the terrorists out of population centers, they're giving families in liberated Iraqi cities a look at a decent and hopeful life.

Our troops are seeing this progress that is being made on the ground. And as they take the initiative from the enemy, they have a question: Will their elected leaders in Washington pull the rug out from under them just as they're gaining momentum and changing the dynamic on the ground in Iraq? Here's my answer is clear: We'll support our troops, we'll support our commanders, and we will give them everything they need to succeed.

Despite the mistakes that have been made, despite the problems we have encountered, seeing the Iraqis through as they build their democracy is critical to keeping the American people safe from the terrorists who want to attack us. It is critical work to lay the foundation for peace that veterans have done before you all.

The Struggles of Democracy

A free Iraq is not going to be perfect. A free Iraq will not make decisions as quickly as the country did under the dictatorship. Many are frustrated by the pace of progress in Baghdad, and I can understand this. As I noted, the Iraqi government is distributing oil revenues across its provinces despite not having an oil revenue law on its books, that the parliament has passed about 60 pieces of legislation.

Prime Minister Maliki is a good guy, a good man with a difficult job, and I support him. And it's not up to politicians in Washington, D.C. to say whether he will remain in his position—that is up to the Iraqi people who now live in a democracy, and not a dictatorship. A free Iraq is not going to transform the Middle East overnight. But a free Iraq will be a massive defeat for al Qaeda, it will be an example that provides hope for millions throughout the Middle East, it will be a friend of the United States, and it's going to be an important ally in the ideological struggle of the 21st century.

Prevailing in this struggle is essential to our future as a nation. And the question now that comes before us is this: Will today's generation of Americans resist the allure of retreat, and will we do in the Middle East what the veterans in this room did in Asia?

The journey is not going to be easy. . . . At the outset of the war in the Pacific, there were those who argued that freedom had seen its day and that the future belonged to the hard men in Tokyo. A year and a half before the attack on Pearl Harbor, Japan's Foreign Minister gave a hint of things to come during an interview with a New York newspaper. He said, "In the battle between democracy and totalitarianism the latter adversary will without question win and will control the world. The era of democracy is finished, the democratic system bankrupt."

In fact, the war machines of Imperial Japan would be brought down—brought down by good folks who only months before had been students and farmers and bank clerks and factory hands. . . .

That generation of Americans taught the tyrants a telling lesson: There is no power like the power of freedom and no soldier as strong as a soldier who fights for a free future for his children. And when America's work on the battlefield was done, the victorious children of democracy would help our defeated enemies rebuild, and bring the taste of freedom to millions.

The Greatest Weapon Against Terrorism

We can do the same for the Middle East. Today the violent Islamic extremists who fight us in Iraq are as certain of their cause as the Nazis, or the Imperial Japanese, or the Soviet Communists were of theirs. They are destined for the same fate.

The greatest weapon in the arsenal of democracy is the desire for liberty written into the human heart by our Creator. So long as we remain true to our ideals, we will defeat the extremists in Iraq and Afghanistan. We will help those countries' peoples stand up functioning democracies in the heart of the broader Middle East. And when that hard work is done and the critics of today recede from memory, the cause of freedom will be stronger, a vital region will be brighter, and the American people will be safer.

> "Political change is nothing we need to
> force upon people; it's something that
> will happen anyway."

The United States Should Not Promote Democracy in the Middle East

Part I: Robert D. Kaplan, Part II: Peter Berkowitz

Both parts of the following viewpoint explore the impact of a U.S. foreign policy that emphasizes democratization of non-democratic states in the Middle East. In Part I, Robert D. Kaplan, national correspondent for the Atlantic Monthly, *argues that forcing democratic reform upon existing Middle Eastern governments has the potential to create greater instability in the region. He maintains that while the leadership in many of the countries there is oppressive, new democratic leadership would not necessarily yield increased peace and security. In Part II, Peter Berkowitz, a fellow at the Hoover Institution on War, Revolution, and Peace at Stanford University, further explores this idea and calls for the promotion of liberty instead of democracy. He contends that many individuals in the Arab world see the forceful imposition of democracy upon sovereign countries to be a critique of Arab ways of life and government. Berkowitz concludes that if the United States shifts to a policy that promotes the principles of liberty such as free speech, free market economics, and an independent judicial system, democracy will naturally follow.*

As you read, consider the following questions:

1. What examples of "moderate and enlightened" Middle Eastern states does Kaplan give?
2. Based on the lessons of Iraq, how does Kaplan believe the United States should handle other despotic regimes?
3. According to Berkowitz, what is the best way to "make democracy stable"?

The whiff of incipient anarchy in Iraq has provided a prospect so terrifying as to concentrate the minds of Republicans and Democrats, Iraq's sectarian political factions, and even the media. Staring over the abyss, only the irresponsible few appear distracted by partisan advantage. In that sense alone, the bombing of the golden dome in Samarra may serve a useful purpose. For the fundamental nightmare of the new century is the breakdown of order, something that the American experience offers precious little wisdom in dealing with.

President [George W.] Bush has posited that the American experience with democracy is urgently useful to the wider world. True, but there is another side of the coin: that America basically inherited its institutions from the Anglo-Saxon tradition and thus its experience over 230 years has been about limiting despotic power rather than creating power from scratch. Because order is something we've taken for granted, anarchy is not something we've feared. But in many parts of the world, the experience has been the opposite, and so is the challenge: how to create legitimate, functioning institutions in utterly barren landscapes.

The Moral Despotic State

"[B]efore the names of Just and Unjust can have place, there must be some coercive power," Thomas Hobbes wrote in *Leviathan* [a book written in 1651 about the construction of the ideal society and government]. Without something or somebody to monopolize the use of force and decide right from wrong, no man is safe from another and there can be no freedom for anyone. Physical security remains the primary human freedom. And so the fact that a state is despotic does not necessarily make it immoral. That is the essential fact of the Middle East that those intent on enforcing democracy abroad forget.

For the average person who just wants to walk the streets without being brutalized or blown up by criminal gangs, a despotic state that can protect him is more moral and far more useful than a democratic one that cannot. Monarchy was the preferred political ideal for centuries, writes the late University of Chicago scholar Marshall Hodgson, precisely because the monarch's legitimacy—coming as it did from God—was seen as so beyond reproach that he could afford to be benevolent, while still monopolizing the use of force. To wit, the most moderate and enlightened states in the Middle East in recent decades have tended to be those ruled by royal families whose longevity has conferred legitimacy: Morocco, Jordan, the Gulf emirates and even Egypt, if one accepts that Hosni Mubarak is merely the latest in a line of Nasserite pharaohs.

Imperfect these rulers clearly are, but to think that who would follow them would necessarily be as stable, or as enlightened, is to engage in the kind of speculation that leads to irresponsible foreign policy. Recall that those who cheered in 1979 at the demise of the shah of Iran got something worse in return. The Saudi Arabian royal family may be the most reactionary group to run that country, except for any other that might replace it. It is unclear what, if anything, besides the monarchy could hold such a geographically ill-defined country together.

Toppling Regimes Creates Instability

In the case of Iraq, the state under Saddam Hussein was so cruel and oppressive it bore little relationship to all these other dictatorships. Because under Hussein anybody could and in fact did disappear in the middle of the night and was tortured in the most horrific manner, the Baathist state constituted a form of anarchy masquerading as tyranny. The decision to remove him was defensible, while not providential. The portrait of Iraq that has emerged since his fall reveals him as the Hobbesian nemesis who may have kept in check an even greater anarchy than the kind that obtained under his rule.

The lesson to take away is that where it involves other despotic regimes in the region—none of which is nearly as despotic as Hussein's—the last thing we should do is actively precipitate their demise. The more organically they evolve and dissolve, the less likely it is that blood will flow. That goes especially for Syria and Pakistan, both of which could be Muslim Yugoslavias in the making, with regionally based ethnic groups that have a history of dislike for each other. The neoconservative yearning to topple Bashar al-Assad [President of Syria], and the liberal one to undermine Pervez Musharraf [President of Pakistan when this article was written; he resigned August 18, 2008, in response to threats of impeachment], are equally adventurous.

Afghanistan falls into none of these categories. We toppled a movement in Afghanistan, the Taliban, but we did not topple a state, because none had really existed there. Even at the high-water mark of central control in Afghanistan in the mid-20th century, the state barely functioned beyond the major cities and the ring road connecting them. The governing self-sufficiency of Afghan villages has been a factor helping President Hamid Karzai establish a legitimate, noncoercive order.

Democratization Cannot Be Forced

Globalization and other dynamic forces will continue to rid the world of dictatorships. Political change is nothing we need to force upon people; it's something that will happen anyway. What we have to work toward—for which peoples with historical experiences different from ours will be grateful—is not democracy but normality. Stabilizing newly democratic regimes, and easing the development path of undemocratic ones, should be the goal for our military and diplomatic establishments. The more cautious we are in a world already in the throes of tumultuous upheaval, the more we'll achieve.

Sometimes President George [W.] Bush and those who side with his post-9/11 refocusing of American foreign policy speak of promoting democracy. On other occasions, the president and those who stand with him talk about spreading liberty. In the United States, we tend to hear these missions as synonymous. In the long run, they no doubt converge. But in the here and now, in dealing with allies and adversaries, they point to different priorities, and distinguishing between them can contribute to a more effective foreign policy.

Why Liberty Must Be Promoted over Democracy

Recent visits to Kuwait and Israel brought home the difference. In early May [2006], among Kuwaiti students, faculty, and university administrators, I heard considerable support for the U.S.-led coalition's removal of Saddam Hussein and efforts to bring democracy to Iraq. But I also heard doubts and anxieties about democracy promotion as a general U.S. strategy for the region. In no small measure this was because the president's policy seemed to imply to my Kuwaiti interlocutors

Democracies Do Not Prevent Terrorism

This view [Middle East democracy is the cure for Islamist terrorism] is rooted in a simplistic assumption: Stagnant, repressive Arab regimes create positive conditions for the growth of radical Islamist groups, which turn their sights on the United States because it embodies the liberal sociopolitical values that radical Islamists oppose. More democracy, therefore, equals less extremism.

History tells a different story. Modern militant Islam developed with the founding of the Muslim Brotherhood in Egypt in the 1920s, during the most democratic period in that country's history. Radical political Islam gains followers not only among repressed Saudis but also among some Muslims in Western democracies, especially in Europe. The emergence of radical Islamist groups determined to wreak violence on the United States is thus not only the consequence of Arab autocracy. It is a complex phenomenon with diverse roots, which include U.S. sponsorship of the mujahideen in Afghanistan in the 1980s (which only empowered Islamist militants); the Saudi government's promotion of radical Islamic educational programs worldwide; and anger at various U.S. policies, such as the country's stance on the Arab-Israeli conflict and the basing of military forces in the region.

Marina Ottaway and Thomas Carothers,
"Think Again: Middle East Democracy,"
Foreign Policy, *November-December 2004.*

the need for fundamental change in Kuwait itself. After all, notwithstanding its elected parliament and its breakthrough decision this spring to grant women the right to vote and run for office, Kuwait remains a constitutional monarchy.

A few weeks later in Israel a retired career army intelligence officer made a similar point. "Why should Israel be eager to see democracy promoted in the region?" he asked. Look at Jordan to the east. King Abdullah is Western educated. He maintains friendly, cooperative relations with Israel and the United States. He rules his people in a generally progressive spirit, with very likely more progressive results than if his kingdom were replaced by a democracy. And what about Egypt, the former intelligence officer continued. Sure, Hosni Mubarak is a dictator, but the dictator we know is preferable to the democracy we don't. Or rather he is preferable to the democracy the Israelis could reasonably anticipate. Mubarak has brought a quarter-century of stability to Israeli-Egyptian relations. Weakening his hold on power, given the poverty, illiteracy, unemployment, and popular appeal of the militant Muslim Brotherhood among the approximately 70 million Egyptians, could well unleash anarchy.

Common to the Kuwaiti and Israeli misgivings is the equation of a policy of democracy promotion with the revolutionary goal of regime change. And this is natural enough. The Bush doctrine is indissolubly connected to Iraq, where an elective war forcibly removed a dictator and undertook the laborious work—on which the jury is still out—of creating democracy almost from scratch. Moreover, by its very name democracy indicates not merely an ethos or a set of procedures but rather a distinctive form of government. In contrast, liberty names a good that can be achieved gradually, one reform at a time, in a variety of regimes. In principle it is possible to secure a considerable range of individual rights in a stable, benevolent monarchy, and sometimes, as in Kuwait and Jordan, more liberty is achievable in the short term than one could reasonably hope to secure through democracy. This is not to doubt the close connection between liberty and democracy. Indeed, they bring out the best in each other.

Shifting the Rhetoric

Over the long haul, the best way to make democracy stable and just is to practice toleration, establish an independent judiciary, encourage a free press, and build a market economy—hallmark liberal institutions all. At the same time, the experience of the last 250 years demonstrates that the best way to secure individual rights is to make government accountable to the people by grounding it in a regular cycle of free and fair elections. And liberty and democracy intertwine in the idea that participating in the choice of government officials is itself an important expression of individual freedom. At the same time, it is useful to keep in mind that instituting majority rule and expanding individual rights are separable undertakings.

Whatever is in our minds when we utter the phrases, democracy promotion proclaims a radical cure—regime change—while spreading liberty suggests incremental reform. Accordingly, concentrating on spreading liberty should be much less threatening to our friends than trumpeting democracy promotion. The same holds true for our adversaries. How, for example, can we effectively engage Iran's government when our grand strategy openly calls for its removal, as it surely does when we put democracy promotion first? Indeed, given the hand the Iranian mullahs are playing, it is, alas, reasonable for them to defy the international community, break their agreements, and accelerate the production of nuclear weapons. What else can provide a deterrent to the United States' declared intention, embodied in the goal of democracy promotion, to sweep the mullahs from power, dismantle their government, and create a new free and fairly elected one?

Concentrating on liberty involves a shift of rhetoric and a change of emphasis in practice. The focus of both, particularly in the wider Middle East, should be in the array of diplomatic and developmental means at our disposal to expand the range of individual rights, particularly liberty of thought and discussion; extending the rule of law; fostering religious toleration;

and ensuring equality of opportunity for women in politics and in the marketplace. Proponents of democracy promotion should not be disappointed or alarmed. One advantage to putting the spread of liberty abroad first in the here and now is the long-term gains it promises in promoting democracy around the globe.

> *"The situation could not be any worse and . . . the American presence in Iraq is causing as much conflict as it is preventing."*

U.S. Troops Should Pull Out of Iraq

Bruce Bartlett

Bruce Bartlett served in both the Ronald Reagan and George H.W. Bush presidential administrations. He is also the author of the book Imposter: How George W. Bush Bankrupted America and Betrayed the Reagan Legacy. *In the following viewpoint he contends that, in retrospect, the invasion of Iraq was a mistake, even though he initially supported George W. Bush's call for military intervention. Bartlett argues that because there is no succinct plan for how to continue the war nor a definition as to what victory would entail, the United States should pull its troops out of Iraq as soon as possible.*

As you read, consider the following questions:

1. For what reasons did the author initially support the war in Iraq, and what information forced him to later change his mind?

Bruce Bartlett, "Good Reasons to Leave Iraq," *The Right Stuff: a New York Times blog*, January 16, 2007. Copyright © 2007 by The New York Times Company. Reprinted with permission.

2. Bartlett states that he doesn't see how the troop surge could be a success based on what two pieces of information?

3. According to the author, how would former President Ronald Reagan have handled the threat of Iraq?

Foreign policy isn't my specialty, but before the Iraq war began I wrote a column cautiously endorsing it *on the basis of what I knew at that time*. There was no pressure on me to say anything on the subject, and I could easily have waited to see how the war turned out before offering an opinion. But that seemed cowardly. Given the importance of the issue, I felt that all opinion leaders had a responsibility to state their views beforehand and not pretend to have always been on the side that history eventually endorses.

Retracting a Misinformed Opinion

I was strongly influenced by reports of weapons of mass destruction [W.M.D.'s] that later turned out to be false. Although I was in no position to evaluate the validity of these reports, there were many experts who deemed them credible. Furthermore, Saddam Hussein's actions in denying United Nations inspectors access to potential locations for W.M.D.'s strongly supported the existence of such weapons.

I finally concluded that if your mortal enemy is pointing a gun at you, you are not obliged to check to make sure that the gun is loaded before defending yourself. It was on this basis that I thought the war just barely passed the threshold of legitimacy. This doesn't mean I would have gone to war if the decision had been mine, only that I was willing to give President [George W.] Bush the benefit of a doubt.

By August 2003, I warned that the Iraq invasion was looking more like a war for empire than self-defense. I finally denounced the war in an April 2004 column and expressed dismay that the administration's justification for it had shifted from W.M.D.'s—which had been a reasonable, if incorrect, basis for war—to liberating the Iraqi people. If Bush had from the beginning justified the war only on grounds of liberation, there would have been no war because there would have been close to zero support for it.

The Need for Disengagement

This still leaves the question of what to do now that we are in Iraq. Just because the war was wrong in the first place doesn't necessarily justify an immediate pullout. There is danger this could make a bad situation worse might embolden our enemies and invite new attacks. That is why I have hesitated calling for disengagement.

But I have come to the conclusion that the situation could not be any worse and that the American presence in Iraq is causing as much conflict as it is preventing. Therefore, I think we should disengage as rapidly as possible. Adding additional troops, as Bush plans to do, simply means throwing good money after bad.

Perhaps if Bush still had any credibility, I would be willing to give him the benefit of a doubt, as I did four years ago. But since then, we have learned how incredibly poor the prewar intelligence was, how Bush essentially bullied intelligence analysts into giving him the reports he wanted, and how he undertook the war with insufficient forces and without giving any thought to postwar planning or an exit strategy.

No Definition for Victory

At this point, it is obvious even to Bush that the status quo is untenable, and he has put the last of his chips on the table to try to salvage something he can call a victory. But there still is no realistic plan for achieving it—or even a definition of victory in the context of Iraq. Consequently, I don't see how this troop surge can possibly succeed. All it will do is put off the

A U.S. Withdrawal from Iraq Will Increase Stability

Serious discussion today [2008] must be about how to deal with the repercussions of the tragic error of the [Iraq] invasion. The key to thinking clearly about it is to give regional stability higher priority than some fantasy victory in Iraq. The first step toward restoring that stability is the complete withdrawal of U.S. forces from Iraq. Only then will promising next steps be possible. . . .

Fear of the chaos that a U.S. withdrawal would catalyze is the psychological block that prevents most observers from assessing the realities clearly. As such observers rightly claim, the United States will be blamed for this chaos, but they overlook the reality that the U.S. military presence now causes much of the chaos and has been doing so since 2003. The United States cannot prevent more chaos by remaining longer. Preventing it is simply not an option. The United States can, however, remove the cause of disorder by withdrawing its forces sooner rather than later. That is the only responsible option. . . .

Most critical in the long run is recognizing that the primary U.S. strategic interest in this part of the world was and still is regional stability. That means subordinating the outcome in Iraq to the larger aim. Getting out of the paralysis in Iraq, chaotic or not, is the sine qua non ["indespensible action"] of any sensible strategy for restoring regional stability.

Colin H. Kahl and William E. Odom,
"When to Leave Iraq? Today, Tomorrow, or Yesterday?"
Foreign Affairs, *July-August 2008.*

inevitable pullout by another year or more, which means that hundreds more of our fighting men and women will die in vain.

I think Bush should have the courage to do what Ronald Reagan did in Lebanon. Reagan sent American troops into that country as part of a multinational peacekeeping force in 1982. But after the situation continued to deteriorate and, in October of 1983, 241 Marines were killed when a truck loaded with explosives blew up outside their barracks, Reagan pulled out.

At the peak of the Cold War, this was a very hard thing for Reagan to do. He knew it would show weakness and undermine his position in dealing with the Soviet Union. But he realized, as Bush does not, that you cannot undo a mistake by continuing to make it. All you can do is stop making the mistake, cut your losses and move on.

What Reagan Would Do

About a year ago [2006], I was on Chris Matthews's television show, and he asked whether I thought Reagan would have gone into Iraq. Not having thought about it ahead of time, I gave a poor answer. I said that I believed he would have if he thought Iraq had W.M.D.'s.

I now realize that my answer was wrong. I don't think Reagan would have invaded Iraq. I think he would have been far more careful than Bush was to make sure the intelligence was right. The debate among Reagan's advisers would have been much more open, with those opposed to invasion getting a fairer hearing. Also, he would have been much more careful to make sure that we had in place a realistic plan for victory, sufficient forces to do the job, a detailed postwar blueprint, and a clear exit strategy, none of which we have had in Iraq.

More important, I think Reagan would have gone much further than Bush did to exhaust all means of dealing with Hussein before even considering going to war. Reagan would have been far more aggressive about using diplomacy backed up by sanctions and air power. Rather than put American troops in harm's way, Reagan would have opted for a surgical strike against Hussein, such as the one he attempted against Muammar el-Qaddafi of Libya in 1986. As he did in Nicaragua and Afghanistan, Reagan would have aided those Iraqis opposed to Hussein and allowed them to do the fighting on the ground. I don't think there is any chance that Reagan would have supported a full-scale military invasion.

It's too late to undo the damage caused by this ill-conceived war. But at least we can stop doing more damage to Iraq and ourselves. I hope Congress finds a way to force Bush to face reality and end the Iraq operation as quickly as possible.

> *"Despite our tragic lapses, leaving [Iraq]*
> *now would be a monumental mis-*
> *take—and one that we would all too*
> *soon come to regret."*

U.S. Troops Should Stay in Iraq

Victor Davis Hanson

In the viewpoint that follows, Victor Davis Hanson argues that the frequent comparisons of the Iraq and Vietnam wars could wrongly lead the American government to pull armed forces from the fight prematurely. However, he maintains that comparisons of the two conflicts are accurate in predicting the negative consequences that would result from an early withdrawal. Hanson states that if U.S. troops leave Iraq before it is secure, the country will be plunged into increasing and continuing violence, leaving the country less stable than when the United States first intervened. Victor Davis Hanson is a military historian with the Hoover Institution at Stanford University and author of the book A War Like No Other.

As you read, consider the following questions:

1. What consequences does the author warn are imminent if U.S. troops leave Iraq before the country is stabilized?

Victor Davis Hanson, "Iraq: Why We Must Stay," *Washington Post*, September 4, 2005, p. B01. Copyright © 2005 Washington Post. Reproduced by permission of the author.

2. According to the author, which countries exemplify American post-war reconstruction successes and which exemplify American post-war reconstruction failures?

3. What are some of the positive influences of the American presence in Iraq, as argued by Hanson?

Vietnam is once again in the air. . . .

America's most contentious war is being freely evoked to explain the "quagmire" we are supposedly now in. Vietnam is an obvious comparison given the frustration of asymmetrical warfare and savage enemies who escape our conventional power. But make no mistake, Iraq is not like Vietnam, and it must not end like Vietnam. Despite our tragic lapses, leaving now would be a monumental mistake—and one that we would all too soon come to regret.

The Consequences of Early Withdrawal

If we fled precipitously, moderates in the Middle East could never again believe American assurances of support for reform and would have to retreat into the shadows—or find themselves at the mercy of fascist killers. Jihadists would swell their ranks as they hyped their defeat of the American infidels. Our forward strategy of hitting terrorists hard abroad would be discredited and replaced by a return to the pre-9/11 [2001] tactics of a few cruise missiles and writs. And loyal allies in Eastern Europe, the United Kingdom, Australia and Japan, along with new friends in India and the former Soviet republics, would find themselves leaderless in the global struggle against Islamic radicalism.

The specter of Vietnam will also turn on those who embrace it. Iraq is not a surrogate theater of the Cold War, where national liberationists, fueled by the romance of radical egalitarianism, are fortified by nearby Marxist nuclear patrons. The jihadists have an 8th-century agenda of gender apartheid, religious intolerance and theocracy. For all its pyrotechnics, the call for a glorious return to the Dark Ages has found no broad constituency.

Nor is our army in Iraq conscript, but volunteer and professional. The Iraqi constitutional debate is already light-years ahead of anything that emerged in Saigon. And there is an exit strategy, not mission creep—we will consider withdrawal as the evolution to a legitimate government continues and the Iraqi security forces grow.

Foreshadowing Defeat

But the comparison to Vietnam may be instructive regarding another aspect—the aftershocks of a premature American departure. Leaving Vietnam to the Communists did not make anyone safer. The flight of the mid-1970s energized U.S. enemies in Iran, Cambodia. Afghanistan and Central America, while tearing our own country apart for nearly a quarter-century. Today, most Americans are indeed very troubled over the war in Iraq—but mostly they are angry about not winning quickly, rather than resigned to losing amid recriminations.

We forget that once war breaks out, things usually get far worse before they get better. We should remember that 1943, after we had entered World War II, was a far bloodier year than 1938, when the world left Hitler alone. Similarly, 2005 may have brought more open violence in Iraq than was visible during Saddam's less publicized killings of 2002. So it is when extremists are confronted rather than appeased. But unlike the time before the invasion, when we patrolled Iraq's skies while Saddam butchered his own with impunity below, there is now a hopeful future for Iraq.

It is true that foreign terrorists are flocking into the country, the way they earlier crossed the Pakistani border into Afghanistan to fight with the Taliban, and that this makes the short-term task of securing the country far more difficult. But again, just as there were more Nazis and fascists out in the open in 1941 than before the war, so too there were almost none left by 1946. If we continue to defeat the jihadists in Iraq—and the untold story of this war is that the U.S. military has performed brilliantly in killing and jailing tens of thousands of them—their cause will be discredited by the stick of military defeat and the carrot of genuine political freedom.

A History of Successful Reconstruction

All this is not wishful thinking. The United States has an impressive record of military reconstruction and democratization following the defeat of our enemies—vs. the abject chaos that followed when we failed to help fragile postwar societies.

After World War II, Germany, Italy and Japan (American troops are still posted in all three) proved to be success stories. In contrast, an unstable post-WWI Weimar Germany soon led to something worse than Kaiser Wilhelm.

After the Korean War, South Korea survived and evolved. South Vietnam, by contrast, ended up with a Stalinist government, and the world watched the unfolding tragedy of the boat people, reeducation camps and a Southeast Asian holocaust.

Present-day Kabul has the most enlightened constitution in the Middle East. Post-Soviet Afghanistan—after we ceased our involvement with the mujaheddin resistance—was an Islamic nightmare.

So we fool ourselves if we think that peace is the natural order of things, and that it follows organically from the cessation of hostilities. It does not. Leave Iraq and expect far worse tribal chaos and Islamic terrorism than in Mogadishu or Lebanon; finish the task and there is the real chance for something like present-day Turkey or the current calm of federated Kurdistan.

An Improvement from the Rule of Saddam Hussein

Have we forgotten that Iraq before the invasion was not just another frightening Middle East autocracy like Syria or Libya, but a country in shambles—not, as some will say, because of international sanctions, but thanks to one of the worst regimes on the planet, with a horrific record of genocide at home and regional aggression abroad? As the heart of the ancient caliphate, Iraq symbolized the worst aspects of pan-Arab nationalism and posed the most daunting obstacle for any change in the Middle East. Thus, al Qaedists and ex-Baathists alike are desperate to drive us out. They grasp that should a democratic Iraq emerge, then the era of both Islamic theocracies and fascist autocracies elsewhere in the region may also be doomed.

Our presence in Iraq is one of the most principled efforts in a sometimes checkered history of U.S. foreign policy. Yes, there is infighting among the Kurds, the Shiites and the Sunnis, but this is precisely because Saddam Hussein pitted the sects against each other for 30 years in order to subjugate them, while we are now trying to unite them so that they might govern themselves. The United States has elevated the formerly despised and exploited Shiites and Kurds to equal status with the Sunnis, their former rulers. And from our own history we know that such massive structural reform is always messy, dangerous—and humane.

So, too, with other changes. It is hard to imagine that Syria would have withdrawn from Lebanon without American resolve in both Afghanistan and Iraq. Nor would either Pakistan's A.Q. Khan or Libya's Moammar Gaddafi have given up on plans to nuclearize the Middle East. Saddam's demise put pressure on Hosni Mubarak to entertain the possibility of democratic reform in Egypt. These upheavals are, in the short term, controversial and volatile developments whose ultimate success hinges only on continued American resolve in Iraq.

Premature Withdrawal from Iraq Would Result in Increased Iraqi Casualties

A reduction in the U.S. combat presence would probably produce one clear benefit: a lower U.S. casualty rate. But a chilling truth is that as the U.S. death toll declined, the Iraqi one would almost surely soar. Just how many Iraqis would die if the U.S. withdrew is anyone's guess, but almost everyone who has studied it believes the current [July 2007] rate of more than a thousand a month would spike dramatically. It might not resemble Rwanda, where more than half a million people were slaughtered [during the genocide there] in six months in 1994. But Iraq could bleed like the former Yugoslavia did from 1992 to 1995, when 250,000 perished [during the Bosnian War].

There is no debate about why: in the wake of an American pullout, Baghdad would be quickly dominated by Shi'ite militias largely unbloodied by the American campaign. Already, well-armed security forces that pose as independent are riddled with militiamen who take direction from Shi'ite leaders. Death-squad killings of Sunnis would rise. Against such emboldened forces, Sunni insurgents and elements of Saddam Hussein's former regime would retaliate with their weapon of choice: car-bomb attacks against Shi'ite markets, shrines, police stations and recruiting depots. . . .

Michael Duffy, "How to Leave Iraq," Time, July 19, 2007.

The Only Solution to Terrorism

There is no other solution to either Islamic terrorism of the sort that hit us on Sept. 11, 2001, nor the sort of state fascism that caused the first Gulf War, than the Bush administration's easily caricatured effort to work for a third democratic choice beyond either dictatorship or theocracy. We know that not because of pre-9/11 [2001] neocon pipedreams of "remaking the Middle East," but because for decades we tried almost everything else in vain—from backing monarchs in the Gulf who pumped oil and dictators in Pakistan and Egypt who promised order, to "containing" murderous autocrats like Saddam and ignoring tyrannous theocrats like the Taliban.

Yes, the administration must account to the American people for the radically humanitarian sacrifices of American lives we are making on behalf of the freedom of Kurds and Shiites. It must remind us that we are engaging murderers of a sort not seen since the Waffen SS and the suicide killers off Okinawa. And it must tell us that victory is our only option and explain in detail how and why we are winning.

The *New York Times* recently deplored the public's ignorance of American heroes in Iraq. In fact, there are thousands of them. But in their eagerness to view Iraq through the fogged lens of Vietnam, the media themselves are largely responsible for the public's shameful lack of interest.

While the networks were transfixed by Cindy Sheehan (or was it Aruba?), the United States military, in conjunction with Iraqi forces, was driving out jihadists from Mosul—where the terrorists are being arrested and killed in droves. Lt. Col. Erik Kurilla of the 1st Battalion, 24th Infantry Regiment, who had worked for months to create an atmosphere of mutual understanding on the city's streets, was severely wounded as he led his men to clear out a terrorist hideaway. The jihadist who shot him—who had recently been released from Abu Ghraib—was not killed, but arrested and given medical care by U.S. surgeons.

Not long before he was wounded, Lt. Col. Kurilla had delivered a eulogy for three of his own fallen men. Posted on a military Web site, it showed that he, far better than most of us, knows why America is there:

"You see—there are 26 million people in Iraq whose freedom we are fighting for, against terrorists and insurgents that want a return to power and oppression, or worse, a state of fundamentalist tyranny. Some of whom we fight are international terrorists who hate the fact that in our way of life we can choose who will govern us, the method in which we worship, and the myriad other freedoms we have. We are fighting so that these fanatical terrorists do not enter the sacred ground of our country and we have to fight them in our own backyard."

Amen.

*"Not only do Israel's foreign policy ob-
jectives not coincide with American interests, they actively hurt them."*

The United States' Close Relationship with Israel Is Harmful to U.S. Interests

Chris Hedges

*Chris Hedges argues in the following viewpoint that the close re-
lationship between the United States and Israel does not serve
the interests of either country and actually creates further tension and incites terrorism. He believes that American interests
would be best served if the U.S. government stopped giving Israel
preferential treatment. Chris Hedges is a Pulitzer Prize-winning
journalist who served as the Middle East bureau chief for the*
New York Times, *writes columns regularly concerning issues in
the Middle East, and is the coauthor of the book* Collateral
Damage: America's War Against Iraqi Civilians.

As you read, consider the following questions:

1. How much money does Hedges state the United States
   gives to Israel in direct assistance each year, and what
   percentage of the total U.S. foreign aid budget is this?

Chris Hedges, "A Declaration of U.S. Independence from Israel," *Washington Report on Middle East Affairs*, vol. 27, August 2008, pp. 10–12. Copyright © 2008 American Educational Trust. All rights reserved. Reproduced by permission.

2. Why does the author believe that "U.S. foreign policy in the Middle East is unraveling"?

3. What are some specific examples of foreign policy decisions made by the United States as a result of the Israel lobby?

Israel, without the United States, would probably not exist. The country came perilously close to extinction during the October 1973 war when Egypt, trained and backed by the Soviet Union, crossed the Suez Canal [into Sinai, territory then occupied by Israel] and the Syrians poured in over the Golan Heights[1]. Huge American military transport planes came to the rescue. They began landing every half-hour to refit the battered Israeli army, which had lost most of its heavy armor. By the time the war was over, the United States had given Israel $2.2 billion in emergency military aid.

The intervention, which enraged the Arab world, triggered the OPEC [Organization of Petroleum Exporting Countries, made up of 13 oil exporting countries] oil embargo that for a time wreaked havoc on Western economies. This was perhaps the most dramatic example of the sustained life-support system the United States has provided to the Jewish state.

A Unique Relationship

Israel was born at midnight May 14, 1948. The U.S. recognized the new state 11 minutes later. The two countries have been locked in a deadly embrace ever since.

Washington, at the beginning of the relationship, was able to be a moderating influence. An incensed President Dwight D. Eisenhower demanded and got Israel's withdrawal after the

1. An area between Israel, Syria, Jordan, and Lebanon with a plateau and mountains; this area always belonged to Syria until Israel captured it during the Six-Day War in 1967.

Israelis occupied Gaza[2] in 1956. During the Six-Day War in 1967, Israeli warplanes bombed the USS *Liberty*. The ship, flying the U.S. flag and stationed 15 miles off the Israeli coast, was intercepting tactical and strategic communications from both sides. The Israeli strikes killed 34 U.S. sailors and wounded 171. The deliberate attack froze, for a while, Washington's enthusiasm for Israel. But ruptures like this one proved to be only bumps, soon smoothed out by an increasingly sophisticated and well-financed Israel lobby that set out to merge Israel and American foreign policy in the Middle East.

Israel has reaped tremendous rewards from this alliance. It has been given more than $140 billion in U.S. direct economic and military assistance. It receives about $3 billion in direct assistance annually, roughly one-fifth of the U.S. foreign aid budget. Although most American foreign aid packages stipulate that related military purchases have to be made in the United States, Israel is allowed to use about 25 percent of the money to subsidize its own growing and profitable defense industry. It is exempt, unlike other nations, from accounting for how it spends the aid money. And funds are routinely siphoned off to build new Jewish settlements, bolster the Israeli occupation in the Palestinian territories and construct the security barrier, which costs an estimated $1 million a mile.

The barrier weaves its way through the West Bank, creating isolated pockets of impoverished Palestinians in ringed ghettos. By the time the barrier is finished it will probably in effect seize up to 40 percent of Palestinian land. This is the largest land grab by Israel since the 1967 war. And although the United States officially opposes settlement expansion and the barrier, it also funds them.

2. A strip of land on the Mediterranean Sea, and bordered by Israel and Egypt; the land is not a part of Israel, but is not recognized as its own sovereign nation though it is currently claimed by the Palestinian National Authority to be part of the Palestinian Territories.

The U.S. has provided Israel with nearly $3 billion to develop weapons systems and given Israel access to some of the most sophisticated items in its own military arsenal, including Blackhawk attack helicopters and F-16 fighter jets. The United States also gives Israel access to intelligence it denies to its NATO [North Atlantic Treaty Organization] allies. And when Israel refused to sign the nuclear nonproliferation treaty, the United States stood by without a word of protest as the Israelis built the region's first nuclear weapons program.

The Results of Favoritism

U.S. foreign policy, especially under the current Bush administration, has become little more than an extension of Israeli foreign policy. The United States since 1982 has vetoed 32 Security Council [branch of the United Nations charged with maintaining international peace and security] resolutions critical of Israel, more than the total number of vetoes cast by all the other Security Council members. It refuses to enforce the Security Council resolutions it claims to support. These resolutions call on Israel to withdraw from the occupied territories [those captured during the 1967 Six-Day War including the West Bank].

There is now volcanic anger and revulsion by Arabs at this blatant favoritism. Few in the Middle East see any distinction between Israeli and American policies, nor should they. And when the Islamic radicals speak of U.S. support of Israel as a prime reason for their hatred of the United States, we should listen. The consequences of this one-sided relationship are being played out in the disastrous war in Iraq, growing tension with Iran, and the humanitarian and political crisis in Gaza. It is being played out in Lebanon, where Hezbollah is gearing up for another war with Israel, one most Middle East analysts say is inevitable. The U.S. foreign policy in the Middle East is unraveling. And it is doing so because of this special relationship. The eruption of a regional conflict would usher in a nightmare of catastrophic proportions.

There were many in the American foreign policy establishment and State Department who saw this situation coming. The decision to throw our lot in with Israel in the Middle East was not initially a popular one with an array of foreign policy experts, including President Harry Truman's secretary of state, Gen. George Marshall. They warned there would be a backlash. They knew the cost the United States would pay in the oil-rich region for this decision, which they feared would be one of the greatest strategic blunders of the postwar era. And they were right. The decision has jeopardized American and Israeli security and created the kindling for a regional conflagration.

The Israel Lobby in the United States

The alliance, which makes no sense in geopolitical terms, does make sense when seen through the lens of domestic politics. The Israel lobby has become a potent force in the American political system. No major candidate, Democrat or Republican, dares to challenge it. The lobby successfully purged the State Department of Arab experts who challenged the notion that Israeli and American interests were identical. Backers of Israel have doled out hundreds of millions of dollars to support U.S. political candidates deemed favorable to Israel. They have brutally punished those who strayed, including the first President Bush, who they said was not vigorous enough in his defense of Israeli interests. This was a lesson the next Bush White House did not forget. George W. Bush did not want to be a one-term president like his father.

Israel advocated removing Saddam Hussein from power and currently advocates striking Iran to prevent it from acquiring nuclear weapons. Direct Israeli involvement in American military operations in the Middle East is impossible. It would reignite a war between Arab states and Israel. The

United States, which during the Cold War avoided direct military involvement in the region, now does the direct bidding of Israel while Israel watches from the sidelines. During the 1991 Gulf war, Israel was a spectator, just as it is in the war with Iraq.

President [George W.] Bush, faring dwindling support for the war in Iraq, publicly holds Israel up as a model for what he would like Iraq to become. Imagine how this idea plays out on the Arab street, which views Israel as the Algerians viewed the French colonizers during the war of liberation.

"In Israel," Bush said recently, "terrorists have taken innocent human life for years in suicide attacks. The difference is that Israel is a functioning democracy and it's not prevented from carrying out its responsibilities. And that's a good indicator of success that we're looking for in Iraq."

Americans are increasingly isolated and reviled in the world. They remain blissfully ignorant of their own culpability for this isolation. U.S. "spin" paints the rest of the world as unreasonable, but Israel, Americans are assured, will always be on our side.

The Situation with the Palestinians

Israel is reaping economic as well as political rewards from its lock-down apartheid state. In the "gated community" market it has begun to sell systems and techniques that allow the nation to cope with terrorism. Israel, in 2006, exported $3.4 billion in defense products—well over a billion dollars more than it received in American military aid. Israel has grown into the fourth largest arms dealer in the world. Most of this growth has come in the so-called homeland security sector.

"The key products and services," as Naomi Klein wrote in *The Nation*, "are hi-tech fences, unmanned drones, biometric IDs, video and audio surveillance gear, air passenger profiling and prisoner interrogation systems—precisely the tools and technologies Israel has used to lock in the occupied territories.

The Overriding Influence of the Israel Lobby on Congress

A key pillar of the [Israel] Lobby's effectiveness is its influence in Congress, where Israel is virtually immune from criticism. This in itself is remarkable, because Congress rarely shies away from contentious issues. Where Israel is concerned, however, potential critics fall silent. One reason is that some key members are Christian Zionists like Dick Armey [former Republican congressman from Texas], who said in September 2002: "My No. 1 priority in foreign policy is to protect Israel." One might think that the No. 1 priority for any congressman would be to protect America. There are also Jewish senators and congressmen who work to ensure that U.S. foreign policy supports Israel's interests. . . .

AIPAC [American Israel Public Affairs Committee] itself, forms the core of the Lobby's influence in Congress. Its success is due to its ability to reward legislators and congressional candidates who support its agenda, and to punish those who challenge it. Money is critical to U.S. elections (as the scandal over the lobbyist Jack Abramoff's shady dealings reminds us), and AIPAC makes sure that its friends get strong financial support from the many pro-Israel political action committees. Anyone who is seen as hostile to Israel can be sure that AIPAC will direct campaign contributions to his or her political opponents. AIPAC also organizes letter-writing campaigns and encourages newspaper editors to endorse pro-Israel candidates. . . .

John Mearsheimer and Stephen Walt, "The Israel Lobby,"
Washington Report on Middle East Affairs, *May-June 2006.*

And that is why the chaos in Gaza and the rest of the region doesn't threaten the bottom line in Tel Aviv [the second largest city in Israel], and may actually boost it. Israel has learned to turn endless war into a brand asset, pitching its uprooting, occupation and containment of the Palestinian people as a half-century head start in the 'global war on terror.'"

The United States, at least officially, does not support the occupation and calls for a viable Palestinian state. It is a global player, with interests that stretch well beyond the boundaries of the Middle East, and the equation that Israel's enemies are our enemies is not that simple.

"Terrorism is not a single adversary," John Mearsheimer and Stephen Walt wrote in *The London Review of Books*, "but a tactic employed by a wide array of political groups. The terrorist organizations that threaten Israel do not threaten the United States, except when it intervenes against them (as in Lebanon in 1982). Moreover, Palestinian terrorism is not random violence directed against Israel or 'the West'; it is largely a response to Israel's prolonged campaign to colonize the West Bank and Gaza Strip. More important, saying that Israel and the U.S. are united by a shared terrorist threat has the causal relationship backwards: the U.S. has a terrorism problem in good part because it is so closely allied with Israel, not the other way around."

The Decidedly Pro-Israel Bush White House

Middle Eastern policy is shaped in the United States by those with very close ties to the Israel lobby. Those who attempt to counter the virulent Israeli position, such as former Secretary of State Colin Powell, are ruthlessly slapped down. This alliance was true also during the Clinton administration, with its array of Israeli-first Middle East experts, including special Middle East coordinator Dennis Ross and Martin Indyk, the former deputy director of the American Israel Public Affairs

Committee, AIPAC, one of the most powerful Israel lobbying groups in Washington. But at least people like Indyk and Ross are sane, willing to consider a Palestinian state, however unviable, as long as it is palatable to Israel. The [George W.] Bush administration turned to the far-right wing of the Israel lobby, those who have not a shred of compassion for the Palestinians or a word of criticism for Israel. These new Middle East exports include Elliott Abrams, John Bolton, Douglas Feith, the disgraced I. Lewis "Scooter" Libby, Richard Perle, Paul Wolfowitz and David Wurmser.

Washington was once willing to stay Israel's hand. It intervened to thwart some of its most extreme violations of human rights. This administration, however, has signed on for every disastrous Israeli blunder, from building the security barrier in the West Bank, to sealing off Gaza and triggering a humanitarian crisis, to the ruinous invasion and saturation bombing of Lebanon.

The few tepid attempts by the Bush White House to criticize Israeli actions have all ended in hasty and humiliating retreats in the face of Israeli pressure. When the Israel Defense Forces in April 2002 reoccupied the West Bank, President Bush called on then-Prime Minister Ariel Sharon to "halt the incursions and begin withdrawal." It never happened. After a week of heavy pressure from the Israel lobby and Israel's allies in Congress, meaning just about everyone in Congress, the president gave up, calling Sharon "a man of peace." It was a humiliating moment for the United States, a clear sign of who pulled the strings.

The Reason for U.S. Military Involvement in the Middle East

There were several reasons for the war in Iraq. The desire for American control of oil, the belief that Washington could build puppet states in the region, and a real, if misplaced, fear of Saddam Hussein played a part in the current disaster. But it was also strongly shaped by the notion that what is good for Israel is good for the United States. Israel wanted Iraq neutralized, Israeli intelligence, in the lead-up to the war, gave faulty information to the U.S. about Iraq's alleged arsenal of weapons of mass destruction. And when Baghdad was taken in April 2003, the Israeli government immediately began to push for an attack on Syria. The lust for this attack has waned, in no small part because the Americans don't have enough troops to hang on in Iraq, much less launch a new occupation.

Israel is currently lobbying the United States to launch aerial strikes on Iran, despite the debacle in Lebanon. Israel's iron determination to forcibly prevent a nuclear Iran makes it probable that before the end of the Bush administration an attack on Iran will take place. The efforts to halt nuclear development through diplomatic means have failed. It does not matter that Iran poses no threat to the United States. It does not matter that it does not even pose a threat to Israel, which has several hundred nuclear weapons in its arsenal. It matters only that Israel demands total military domination of the Middle East.

The alliance between Israel and the United States has culminated after 50 years in direct U.S. military involvement in the Middle East. This involvement, which is not furthering American interests, is unleashing a geopolitical nightmare. American soldiers and Marines are dying in droves in a useless war. The impotence of the United States in the face of Israeli pressure is complete. The White House and the Congress have become, for perhaps the first time, a direct extension of Israeli interests. There is no longer any debate within the United States. This is evidenced by the obsequious nods to Israel by all the current presidential candidates with the exception of Dennis Kucinich. The political cost for those who challenge Israel is too high.

The High Cost of the Close U.S.-Israel Relationship

This means there will be no peaceful resolution of the Palestinian-Israeli conflict. It means the incidents of Islamic terrorism against the U.S. and Israel will grow. It means that American power and prestige are on a steep, irreversible decline. And I fear it also means the ultimate end of the Jewish experiment in the Middle East.

The weakening of the United States, economically and militarily, is giving rise to new centers of power. The U.S. economy, mismanaged and drained by the Iraq war, is increasingly dependent on Chinese trade imports and on Chinese holdings of U.S. Treasury securities. China holds dollar reserves worth $825 billion. If Beijing decides to abandon the U.S. bond market, even in part, it would cause a free fall by the dollar. It would lead to the collapse of the $7 trillion U.S. real estate market. There would be a wave of U.S. bank failures and huge unemployment. The growing dependence on China has been accompanied by aggressive work by the Chinese to build alliances with many of the world's major exporters of oil, such as Iran, Nigeria, Sudan and Venezuela. The Chinese are preparing for the looming worldwide dash over dwindling resources.

The future is ominous. Not only do Israel's foreign policy objectives not coincide with American interests, they actively hurt them. The growing belligerence in the Middle East, the calls for an attack against Iran, the collapse of the imperial project in Iraq have all given an opening, where there was none before, to America's rivals. It is not in Israel's interests to ignite a regional conflict. It is not in ours. But those who have their hands on the wheel seem determined, in the name of freedom and democracy, to keep the American ship of state headed at breakneck speed into the cliffs before us.

> *"In this region [the Middle East], one strategic ally in particular has always stood out from all others: the state of Israel."*

The United States' Close Relationship with Israel Is Beneficial to U.S. Interests

Part I: Steve Rothman, Part II: David Frum

In the two parts of the viewpoint that follows, each author constructs an argument as to why the U.S. relationship with Israel is so important to American security. In Part I, New Jersey Congressman Steve Rothman focuses on the strength of Israel in defeating aggressors, and emphasizes the ways in which Israel militarily aids the United States. Part II of the viewpoint, by David Frum, a fellow at the American Enterprise Institute, a conservative think tank, focuses on the reasons why American public support for Israel is so high. He contends that because Israelis share the same values as Americans, the close relationship is apt and necessary.

As you read, consider the following questions:

1. How many more troops does Rothman estimate would be needed in the Middle East if Israel was not a close U.S. ally?

2. At what points has American support for Israel been highest, and at what times has Arab popularity been lowest, based on the statistics from the polls cited by Frum?

3. What are some of the reasons why Americans like Israelis and dislike Arabs, according to Frum?

American foreign policy is front and center in the 2008 presidential election. Eight years of deadly and disastrous blunders by the [George W.] Bush administration have seriously damaged our national readiness and our allegiances throughout the world. Bush's errors range from recklessly launching a war in Iraq on false pretenses to disgracing the 60th anniversary of the state of Israel with a polarizing and political speech before the Israeli Knesset [the Israeli legislature].

The American people recognize that the next president of the United States must do a better job of working with and strengthening our allies, especially those in the Middle East. And it must be understood that in this region, one strategic ally in particular has always stood out from all others: the state of Israel.

Israel Aids the U.S. Military

In the 60 years since America and the United Nations recognized Israel as a sovereign and independent nation, the U.S. has been rewarded tenfold for this gesture by Israel's help in providing America with vital security assistance in the Middle East and around the world.

I remember my first trip to Israel in 1968. I still recall standing amid the rubble of war and burned out Soviet tanks in the Golan Heights, recognizing that this tiny country—nearly the same size as my home state of New Jersey—had accomplished the impossible in defeating the armies of Egypt, Syria and Jordan, as well as forces from Saudi Arabia, Iraq, Lebanon, Kuwait and Algeria.

Today, Israel Defense Forces (IDF) continue to demonstrate great strength and acumen as they protect their people and provide valuable assistance to the U.S. There are literally hundreds of examples of how Israel has helped the United States with our national security goals: intelligence, improving American military technology, capturing Soviet and Iranian equipment, destroying the Iraqi nuclear reactor, eradicating a Syrian nuclear facility, and many more unclassified and classified instances.

Currently, the United States spends $150 billion a year to have 165,000 U.S. combat troops in Iraq.

Many people know that. What they may not realize is that without our partnership with the IDF, the United States might need to have 100,000 or more additional troops stationed permanently in that part of the world to make up for the protection of U.S. interests and vital intelligence provided by Israel to the United States.

The Need for a Mutual Defense Project

With the ongoing efforts of Iran to acquire nuclear weapons technology, it is more critical than ever that the U.S. continue to fund defense programs with Israel to deter common enemies. The Arrow Weapons System is a notable example. Arrow, a joint U.S.-Israel defense project, is one of the most advanced missile defense systems in existence and has been proven effective in tests against real and surrogate targets.

For Israel, Arrow provides essential protection against ballistic missiles for its civilian population, as well as U.S. troops, ships, and aircraft in the Middle East. Specifically, Arrow directly counters the threat posed by hostile Iranian Shahab-3 missiles by intercepting them at high altitudes so that any weapons of mass destruction that they carry will not detonate or be dispersed over Israel or U.S. forces.

The system can detect and track missiles at distances as far as 300 miles away, while also destroying an incoming warhead a safe distance from the target. Arrow's newest component, known as Arrow-3, will improve the Arrow System and give it the capability to handle more sophisticated ballistic missile threats from Iran, such as multiple warheads and faster reentry vehicles.

In addition, U.S. participation in the Arrow development effort ensures interoperability [reciprocal use] of the Arrow and Israeli Missile Defense system with deployed U.S. missile defense assets. To grasp the magnitude of that benefit, think about how important it is for our first responders—fire, police and emergency medical services—to be on the same page when responding to a crisis. Their response times are increased, effectiveness is magnified, and the likelihood of miscommunication errors is decreased.

Israeli and U.S. Security Closely Linked

Arrow technology, along with other American and Israeli defensive and offensive systems, coupled with robust diplomacy, will protect American interests and allies against threats in the Middle East and help us avert another deadly and costly war.

I will fight for ongoing strong support of an enhanced Arrow System and expect that, as in the past, my colleagues—Democrats and Republicans alike—will join me. Those of us on the Defense Appropriations Subcommittee recognize that our national security interests extend beyond partisan politics.

Our own national security is closely linked to that of Israel, and the American people understand that. I look forward to working with our next president to assure that our long and successful strategic alliance and defense technology partnership with Israel continue and prosper.

Why does the United States support Israel so strongly?

Israel's enemies think they know the answer. It is a conspiracy, the work of a sinister "lobby."

But there's a simpler and more powerful explanation: The American people favour the Jewish state over its enemies—and that support has only intensified with the passage of time.

American Public Opinion of Israel

Israel declared its independence in May, 1948. It was immediately attacked—and Americans were immediately polled on the ensuing war by the National Opinion Research Center [NORC]. Thirty-four per cent of Americans said they sympathized more with the Jews of Palestine; 12% said they sympathized more with the Arabs. (Eytan Gilboa's *American Public Opinion Toward Israel and the Arab-Israeli Conflict* is the source of most of the numbers I'll cite here.)

This 3:1 ratio looks impressive. But still: More than half of all Americans took no view at all. In later NORC surveys, barely one-third of Americans rated the relationship with Israel as "very important."

The polls continue to show coolness to Israel through the 1950s—with more Americans blaming Israel than Egypt for the 1956 war. The great turning point comes in 1967, after the Six-Day War.

June, 1967, polls showed sympathy for Israel surging above the 50% mark for the first time—and sympathy for the Arabs plunging below the 5% mark. An epoch had been turned. Over the next four decades, feelings about the Arab-Israeli dispute would settle and harden, with sympathy for Israel averaging a little above 45% and sympathy for Israel's Arab enemies averaging slightly more than 10%.

Those overall averages concealed fascinating variations. White Americans supported Israel more strongly than African Americans. Educated Americans were more pro-Israel than less educated Americans. And especially since 1982, right-of-

The Exaggerated Importance of the Israel Lobby

Does Israel have supporters in the U.S. that back a strong relationship between the two countries? Clearly, networks of such support exist, as they do for U.S. ties with Britain, Greece, Turkey, and India. There are also states like Saudi Arabia that have tried to tilt U.S. policy using a vast array of powerful PR [public relations] firms, former diplomats, and well-connected officials. The results of those efforts have America still overly dependent on Middle Eastern oil with few energy alternatives. Given the ultimate destination of those petrodollars in recent years (the global propagation of Islamic extremism and terrorism), a serious investigation of those lobbying efforts appears to be far more appropriate than focusing on relations between the U.S. and Israel. . . .

In the last two decades, Americans are finding that the strategic focal point of their military activism is increasingly in the Middle East, particularly with the pacification of Europe after the collapse of the Soviet Union (the Balkan Wars of the 1990s, notwithstanding). This shift from Europe to the Middle East is understandable given the fact that the main global threats to American security—al-Qaeda terrorism and the proliferation of weapons of mass destruction as well as missile delivery systems—now emanate from the Middle East region. . . .

Dore Gold, "Understanding the U.S.-Israel Alliance:
An Israeli Response to the Walt-Mearsheimer Claim,"
Jerusalem Viewpoints, *September 2007.*

centre Americans have tended to become more and more pro-Israel, while left-of-centre Americans have tended to become less so.

Rewarding Competence and Professionalism

Yet underneath all these variations, here's the hard fact. The American public as a whole strongly supports the state of Israel, and this support has only intensified over time.

The so-called Israel lobby succeeds in Washington for exactly the same reason that Mothers Against Drunk Driving has succeeded in their lobbying: because it has public opinion on their side.

The next question is: Why? And to that question, the polling data suggest an answer.

The highest points in Israel's popularity (52% and better) include June, 1967, December, 1973, July–August, 1982, January, 1991, February, 2002, and almost all of the period since 2006.

Conversely, the lowest points in Arab unpopularity (8% and less) include the whole of the period from 1967 through 1973, and most of the period since September, 2001.

The American public does not like terrorism. It did not like the wave of hijackings and murders launched by the Palestine Liberation Organization in 1969, and it does not like the wave of suicide bombings that followed Yasser Arafat's "second intifada" in October, 2000.

The American public does not like unprovoked aggression. It did not like the Egyptian-Syrian sneak attack of October, 1973, it did not like Saddam Hussein's missile attacks on Israel during the Gulf War, and it does not like the rocket attacks on Sderot today.

The American public respects competence and professionalism. Israel's triumph in June, 1967, its come-from-behind victory in 1973, its shooting down of 86 Syrian planes without the loss of one of its own at the opening of the Lebanon war—all these won favorable responses.

Seeing the Truth

Finally: The terror attacks of 9/11 [2001] have convinced many Americans that Israel and the United States stand together. Images of Palestinians dancing on 9/11, the rise of Hamas and Iran's repeated threats of genocide have shaped a new awareness that Israel's enemies are also America's, and America's are also Israel's.

It's often said that perception is reality. It's even more true, however, that reality is perception. Israel's Arab enemies are unpopular because Americans see them for what they are. And Israel is liked because Americans see it for what it is.

Which implies this lesson for those who seek to counteract the power of the "Israel lobby." If Israel's enemies would only disavow genocide, eschew religious extremism, halt terrorism, adopt democracy, practise tolerance, and offer and accept reasonable compromise—then Americans would like them a lot better.

Of course, in that case, it would not matter whether Americans liked them or not—for if Israel's enemies ever did those things, the conflict would be over.

Periodical Bibliography

The following articles have been selected to supplement the diverse views presented in this chapter.

James G. Abourezk   "Resurrecting a Modern Myth: 'The Surge Is Working,'" *Washington Report on Middle East Affairs*, September–October 2008.

Jed Babbin   "Time to Rethink Iraq," *Human Events*, July 21, 2008.

Michael Barone   "We're Not Leaving . . ." *U.S. News & World Report*, July 21, 2008.

Steven A. Cook   "Disentangling Alliances," *American Interest*, September–October 2008.

The Economist   "Leave as Soon as You Sensibly Can," August 30, 2008.

Leon Hadar   "Israel as a U.S. 'Strategic Asset': Myths and Realities," *Middle East Policy*, December 2006.

Scott T. Hadar   "Time for U.S. to Embrace 'Constructive Disengagement' from the Mideast," *Energy Tribune*, August 2008.

Shadi Hamid   "Vision Gap, Part II: The Case for Putting Democracy Promotion at the Center of a New Progressive Foreign Policy Vision," *American Prospect*, August 24, 2006. www.prospect.org.

Glenn Kessler   "Fix This Middle Eastern Mess," *Washington Quarterly*, Autumn 2008.

Michael B. Oren   "Israel Is Now America's Closest Ally," *Wall Street Journal*, May 7, 2008.

James Webb   "From Beirut to Bin Laden," *American Conservative*, June 30, 2008.

CHAPTER 2

How Can There Be Peace Between Israel and Palestine?

Chapter Preface

The two-state solution, which calls for the creation of an independent Israeli state and an independent state for Palestine in Gaza and the West Bank, is the most internationally backed plan for bringing about peace between the Israelis and Palestinians. It is also the solution that is currently advocated by the United States. However, negotiating a two-state peace process has been slow and fraught with many impediments.

The chief stumbling block has been the switch in Palestine's ruling party. In the 2006 Palestinian legislative election, Fatah, a somewhat liberal nationalist party, lost its hold on the Palestinian Legislative Council, Palestine's unicameral parliament, to the Islamist group Hamas. Though a popular faction in Palestine, Hamas is internationally regarded as a more radical party known for terrorist acts and strident call for the destruction of Israel. When Hamas took power, global reaction was not favorable. The United States, Russia, the European Union, and the United Nations—those powers that were mediating peace in the region—penalized the Palestinian National Authority by cutting its funding as a sign of disapproval. The United States also backed a coup attempt to overthrow Hamas and bring Fatah back to the fore.

In early 2007, Palestine's president, Mahmoud Abbas, a member of Fatah, agreed to work with the Hamas-led legislature to create a more unified Palestinian government that could carry on the peace process with Israel and hopefully jump start the two-state negotiations. Unfortunately, the resolve of the unity government was shaky at best, and the brief accord fell apart after Hamas militias and Fatah security forces clashed in Gaza in March 2008. Another factor contributing to the decline in hope for a two-state solution is the failure of a six-month cease-fire between Hamas and Israel. Just hours after the resolution was signed in Egypt on June 18, 2008, Israel violated the treaty by firing on fishermen and farmers along the coast of the Gaza Strip. A similar incident was reported on October 5, 2008, when Israeli naval forces opened fire on Palestinian fishing boats in the Gaza Strip, causing increased tensions and threatening the fragile peace negotiations.

Although the two-state solution has not been abandoned, the recent obstacles to the plan have prompted many insiders and outsiders to suggest that a one-state solution may be necessary and perhaps more desirable. Under the one-state, or binational, plan, all Israelis and Palestinians living in Israel, the West bank, and Gaza would be afforded equal citizenship in a unitary country. Many Palestinians favor this resolution, though critics believe that Israelis would not support it. Yossi Alpher, a former adviser in the Israeli government, states that Israelis "would prefer renewed dispersion and Diaspora to life in a binational Arab-Jewish (essentially Muslim-Jewish) state that by definition would not be Zionist and would almost certainly quickly relegate Jews to the status of a persecuted minority."

In the following chapter, Michael Tarazi offers his opinion that Israel and Palestine should be a single state because they already function as one, due to their shared infrastructure and because of the growing support of Palestinians for a one-state solution. Other authors in the chapter debate aspects of the Israeli-Palestinian peace process beyond the one- or two-state solutions.

> "We are in search of a political will to
> bring about the two parties to finally
> make the deal [for peace]."

Peace Negotiations Between Israel and Palestine Are Possible

Marwan Muasher

The Israeli-Palestinian conflict has been the catalyst for great discontent throughout the Arab world. In the viewpoint that follows, former deputy prime minister of Jordan, Marwan Muasher, contests the idea that Arab extremists are the only influential force in the Israeli-Palestinian peace process and argues that if a peace agreement is to be reached between the Israelis and Palestinians, the moderate Arab movement must be central in its negotiation. While many fundamentalist Arab groups rally for the destruction of the state of Israel, Muasher believes that a peace agreement between Israelis and Palestinians will benefit both Arabs and Israelis on the whole, creating more stability in the region and allowing the two groups to live peacefully side by side. Marwan Muasher served as an ambassador to Israel following

Marwan Muasher, "Peace Between Arabs and Israel Is Wanted and Possible," *Los Angeles World Affairs Council*, July 10, 2008, pp. 1–5. Reproduced by permission of the author.

the 1994 Oslo Accord and is currently the senior vice president of external affairs at the World Bank. He is also the author of the book The Arab Center.

As you read, consider the following questions:

1. Why, according to Muasher, are moderate Arabs viewed as failures within the Arab community?
2. For what two reasons, in the author's view, are radical groups such as Hezbollah and Hamas so popular in the Arab world?
3. Muasher states that a peaceful solution to the Israeli-Palestinian conflict is in the interest of both Israel and the Arab world for what simple reason?

Today, to be a moderate in the Arab world has been described as a leap of faith, an act of courage, or sometimes just plain suicidal. But there has never been a time when moderation is more needed in our region than it is today. . . .

Most Arab politicians kiss and don't tell. They are in office for a long time and when they leave, whether it's because they don't want to upset anyone or because they do want to go back to government, they choose not to document their experiences. Therefore, most of the history of our region in the Arab world has been written by outsiders. Of those who do document few do so in English. . . .

The Moderate Arab Position

On peace the Western world tends to focus on Arab extremists. But at least that on the issue of peace there is an Arab center. Not only is there an Arab center but an Arab center that has been proactive and that has put on the table all the initiatives of this decade to peacefully end the Arab-Israeli conflict. It did that after a heated debate with the radical elements of the Arab world. It won the day, and starting with the Arab Peace Initiative of 2002, the Arab moderate position prevailed in putting on the table a peace proposal that would commit, not Arab states neighboring Israel, but the whole of the Arab world to a peace treaty with Israel. And the strength of the Arab peace initiative of 2002, which started with Saudi Crown Prince Abdullah, was the notion that for Israel to grant some painful concessions on its part, the idea of a separate agreement with the Palestinians might not give Israel the security that it needs in order to sign the peace treaty. Therefore, rather than push for a separate peace treaty between Israel and the Palestinians or Israel and the Syrians, the Arab Peace Initiative put on the table a proposal that in return for the end of the occupation of Arab land the whole Arab world—the whole Arab world—would commit itself to a collective peace treaty with Israel; to collective security guarantees with Israel; and to an end to the conflict with no more claims. I, as an ex-ambassador to Israel, understand perfectly how every Israeli feels about this very point, that after an agreement no Arab would claim pre-1948 Palestine. And the most important offering, an agreed solution to the refugee problem meaning that no Arab claims that four or five million Palestinians would go back to Israel and threaten the demographic nature of the Israeli state—an agreed solution to the refugee problem.

Unfortunately, I think that initiative was not given what it deserved both because the United States was more focused on Iraq and not focused at the time on the Arab-Israeli conflict, and because Israel took the reference in the agreement to mean that the Arabs were talking about sending back four or five million Palestinians when it was clearly not the case. The Arabs did a poor job of marketing the initiative and, therefore, at the time it was not met with strong enthusiasm.

The Arab center went further in 2002-2003 in proposing a plan to translate this vision of a two-state solution into concrete steps. Steps that would start with meeting the security needs of Israel and would end with a political horizon for the Palestinians and the two-state solution. That plan, called the road map, in which Jordan played a key role in developing, did not see any reasonable chance of implementation once the war in Iraq started and once the U.S. efforts were all directed towards that war. And so I argue that if we do not have peace today it is not because of the lack of trying on the part of the Arab moderates. They have been at the forefront of all the peace efforts in this decade. . . .

The Human Side of Conflict

It is easy to write about the conflict in analytical terms, but what people don't always appreciate and understand is the psychological divide that exists sometimes between the two peoples and the leaps of faith that people and countries would have to make for peace to come to the region.

The most difficult week in my life was when King Hussein asked me to become ambassador to Israel. Even though to all of you this would be an extremely great honor, to me, a moderate, a spokesman of the delegation for the negotiations, someone who had dealt with the Israelis for a long time it was still difficult to accept and actually go and live there. I went through a lot of internal struggle, I had to make a leap of faith in order to do that. . . . When President Weizman invited me, as he did all the diplomatic corps, to attend Israel's Independence Day in his garden in west Jerusalem, to me and to all Arabs this was the anniversary of the Arabs' tragedy, of the Arabs' Nakba and the feelings that you go through is an experience when you do that. These are not easy matters but they all point to one fact: that if we are going to let the history of both peoples decide what the future will be there won't be a future and that as rich as both our histories are they cannot be mutually exclusive. If they are, then we cannot have a solution.

Reform in the Arab World

Reform in the Arab world . . . is, in my opinion, one of the principal reasons why the Arab center today is very much on the defensive. We are a dying breed. We are a dying breed because despite our valiant efforts to solve the peace process, we have not solved it. But we are also responsible for not addressing other issues of concern to the Arab society—political reform, good government, economic well-being, cultural diversity. And because the center in the Arab world is a one-issue center—it's focused only on the peace process—not having solved that conflict, it has nothing to show for its efforts and the radical elements in the region are saying, "You have not solved peace when it was your strongest suit, you have not brought peace and you have not addressed reform. Why should we believe you? Maybe the violent track is a better track to take." And today in the Arab world Arab moderates have no counter argument. They are partly responsible, as I said, for not embarking on a serious process of reform in our countries.

Today there are two schools of thought in the Arab world. The traditional school of thought that says if you open up the system the radicals come in and, therefore, the solution is to not open up the political systems in the Arab world. That, of course, ignores the fact that the radicals have not been weakened by the continuation of the closed systems. Who among you heard of Hezbollah or Hamas [Islamic fundamentalist groups opposed to the existence of the Israeli State] 25 years ago? None. And why? Because they did not exist 25 years ago. Today they are not only in existence, they are very popular in the Arab world because they are talking about a violent track, which in their opinion brings results, but they are also talking about good governance. They are providing services for people, and promising cleaner government than the ruling elite. And so, the reformist school in the Arab world says, "We cannot have a system that continues to give two options to people—either a ruling elite with no system of checks and balances, or a radical ideology which promises or which threatens the political and cultural diversity of society." For other alternatives to emerge there is no option but to open up the system in a gradual, yes, in a gradual but also in a serious manner. This is a process that will take 40 or 50 years. It's not a process that can happen over night. It's not something that you can solve with a magic wand, but there is no escaping the fact that unless the political systems are open, the Arab world will continue to lag behind almost every other region of the world in terms of governments.

The United States' Role

What can the United States do on both these issues? There is nothing more that the United States can do to help the cause of the Arab moderates than to bring about an end to the Arab-Israeli conflict. I'm a creature of the Oslo process[1] The Oslo process' principal philosophy was a gradual approach to the Arab-Israeli peacemaking and the notion that when you tackle the easier problems first and you leave the thornier issues to the end, you build confidence among the parties, confidence that will allow both of them to make the painful compromises necessary. What the process ignores is that while the parties are building confidence the opponents of peace on both sides are using this long period of time to derail the process repeatedly and effectively, and they have done so. In these last 15 years of peacemaking—Oslo was supposed to end only after five, the last 15 years of peacemaking the opponents used all this time in order to shatter the confidence that exists between the two parties and today that confidence is at an all-time low. In my opinion any going back to a gradual process is only a gift to the radicals, it's only a gift to those who do not want peace to come to our region. But fortunately, the framework for a solution today exists and it's not a framework that is imposed by a superpower or the United States or anybody else. It is a framework that has already been negotiated among the parties themselves. We only have to look at the

1. A milestone in the Israeli-Palestinian conflict, which occurred in 1993 in Oslo, Norway; it was the first time Palestinian representatives conceded Israeli's right to Statehood.

Clinton parameters, the talks that followed, the Arab Peace Initiative, the Geneva documents—I can name a series of frameworks that have been arrived at among the parties and that have tackled everything from Jerusalem to refugees to borders, to security. And, yes, while I admit that no detailed solutions were arrived at, I still maintain that these frameworks have already defined the outer parameters of a solution and I still maintain that no amount of negotiations will bring us closer to what the parties have already done.

So, we today are not in search of a political framework. We are in search of a political will to bring about the two parties to finally make the deal and there is no one but the United States that can do this. Conventional wisdom in the region had it that the U.S. administration takes the Arab-Israeli conflict in their second term, because the president is speaking of his legacy because, this is the conventional wisdom in the Arab world; he is freer from the Jewish lobby and can make freer decisions, etc. That is not supported by fact. No U.S. president has taken the Arab-Israeli conflict in his second term and succeeded, not one. If you look at all the efforts of President Clinton to solve the conflict or if you look at the current attempts to solve the conflict after seven years of disengagement from the process, these are not going to be successful efforts.

The only successful efforts from U.S. intervention came when the United States took on the Arab-Israeli conflict in a president's first term. Whether it was President Carter in 1978 with the Camp David Accords and the peace treaty between Israel and Egypt, or whether it is President Bush senior and the Madrid Peace Conference, these were all initiatives that were taken in the administrations first term. If there is any suggestion that I would give to either Mr. [John] McCain [2008 Republican presidential candidate] or Mr. [Barack] Obama [2008 Democratic presidential candidate] it is that they should take on the Arab-Israeli conflict in their first

Palestinians Must Unite to End the Occupation

Palestinians are entering a critical stage in their history. More oppressive structures are firmly established now, raising the possibility of permanent dispossession and national disintegration. Geographically and politically divided, Palestinians around the world know neither their immediate goals nor their long-term objectives. Such a deep crisis requires widespread collective engagement and effort. It may be useful to take the recent Palestinian Prisoners' Document of National Conciliation, [written by Palestinian prisoners as they were being held in an Israeli jail] amended and agreed upon by both Fatah and Hamas on June 27, [2006] as a launching pad for emerging debates and discussions. The prisoners clearly call for the end of the occupation, dismantling of all settlements and realization of Palestinian national rights. Their position is supported by a majority of Palestinians in the occupied territories, who realize that it may well prove to be the strongest basis for national unity today. A national liberation movement can achieve success only if it is based on values of self-organization, independence, democracy and active mass participation, including women and workers. A new anticolonial national movement is still possible and ever more necessary. And if the outcome of decolonization also produces a constituency in Israel happy to live in peace and equality with the Palestinians without walls and borders, so much the better. But there's no shortcut around the struggle against the occupation.

Bashir Abu-Manneh, "In Palestine, a Dream Deferred,"
Nation, *November 30, 2006.*

term. They have all the ammunition they need, they have the framework they need for a solution. But if we are to wait until all the stars are properly aligned in the Palestinian camp and in the Israeli camp and in the regional camp we are not going to arrive at a solution.

Reform from the Arab Center

And today, ironically, a solution is as much in Israel's interest as it is in the Arab world's interest. Why? Simply because of the demographic issue. Israel today is a nation of six million Israelis, one million of them are Arabs. If you add to that the 3.8 million Palestinians in the West Bank and Gaza under occupation, you have today a situation where the number of Jews in Israel is almost equal to the number of Arabs. And in a few years time, not in the distant future, the number of Arabs will outnumber the number of Jews. So what will Israel do? If Israel does not opt for a two-state solution and Israel cannot support a one-state solution, in which all people under its control become citizens and thereby destroy the nature of the Jewish state, what option does Israel have? To continue the occupation indefinitely? A two-state solution today is in everybody's interest. It's not a gift that anybody is giving to one side or the other. [Israeli] Prime Minister [Yitzhak] Rabin understood this, understood it very well, and stopped the talking about the Palestinian entity, he did not call it a state, in 1994. And then Mr. Sharon and Mr. Olmert in Israel started talking about the Palestinian state ten years down the road.

What about groups like Hamas and Hezbollah? In my opinion, a separate solution between Israel and the Palestinians today, a separate solution is not possible precisely because in the context of an agreement between Israel and the Palestinians, Israel is going to feel that it is not signing an agreement with the whole of the Palestinian community, that half the Palestinian community does not want an agreement with it and might jeopardize it in one way or another through Hamas. But if Israel signs an agreement with the whole Arab world in which the whole Arab world commits, as it did already with the Arab Peace Initiative, to an agreement, a group such as Hamas becomes a very minor player.

Unfortunately, the United States' support for the reform process in the Arab world in recent years might have been almost the kiss of death because of the perception that there has been a double standard, because of the perception that the United States started pushing very strongly for reform but once it saw that it was also not to its liking it suddenly withdrew. Therefore, reform in the Arab world must be the responsibility of the Arab center, of the Arab moderates, and a homegrown process must be initiated by the Arab center if that center is to be credible and consistent in the Arab world and popular at the same time. Once that happens then I believe the United States and the international community can be supportive of such a process.

Compromises on Both Sides

So, just to sum up. I believe that on the one hand that if Israel wants to be accepted as a member of the neighborhood then it has to work for the rights of the Palestinians to live free of occupation and have their own state. And if the Arab center, if the Arab moderates, are to rid themselves of the image their opponents are painting of them in the Arab world today—of being compromisers of Arab life or apologists for the West— they also must plant the seeds for the time when the peace process will end but the challenge of a pluralistic democratic and prosperous society remains.

> "Israel, which ceaselessly professes its de-
> sire for peace, has never initiated a
> peace proposal of its own."

Peace Negotiations Between Israel and Palestine Are Not Possible

Ghada Karmi

*Ghada Karmi argues in the following viewpoint that the real ob-
stacle to the achievement of a resolution to the Israeli-Palestinian
conflict is Israel. According to the author, Israel continues to
refuse all peace proposals set forth by any party in an attempt to
stall the signing of any agreement. In Karmi's opinion, the Israelis want to continue to colonize Palestinian lands so that it will
be more difficult to return these lands to Palestinian control.
Karmi concludes that as long as Israel disapproves of the peace
proposals, no peace agreement will be reached in the region.
Ghada Karmi is a Palestinian doctor and scholar living in England and active in advocating a one-state solution to the Israeli-*

Palestinian conflict. She is the author of Married to Another Man: Israel's Dilemma in Palestine *and currently an honorary research fellow and assistance lecturer at the University of Exeter in England.*

As you read, consider the following questions:

1. According to Karmi, when did the peace process begin, and how many failures to establish peace have failed since that time?

2. The author states that Israel controls what percentage of land and resources as a result of its barrier wall on the West Bank?

3. What does Karmi argue to be the three possible outcomes of the Israeli-Palestinian conflict?

Everyone wants to see "peace" between Israel and the Arabs. It has now dawned on most people that the terrorist attacks on America and Europe, the al-Qaeda rhetoric about the suffering of fellow Muslims, and the instability in the Middle East are connected with the unresolved Israeli-Palestinian conflict.

The previous British prime minister, Tony Blair, realised this truth while still in office. In his new post as Middle East envoy for the Quartet (the European Union, Russia, the US and the UN [United Nations]), he has put peacemaking in Israel/Palestine at the top of his agenda. The vehicle for this, so beloved of Western policy makers, is the "peace process", a bland term that suggests something is being done while absolving the major players of any responsibility for real thought or action.

The Peace Process History

The peace process began in 1993 with the Oslo Agreement drawn up between then Israeli prime minister Yitzhak Rabin and Palestinian leader Yasser Arafat. The agreement was supposed to eventually resolve the conflict through stages, ending implicitly in the creation of a Palestinian state. Instead, it initiated years of broken agreements and interminable negotiations, all called "the peace process", and ended in 2000 with the second intifada [uprising] and the current crisis.

No attempt was made to confront the causes for Oslo's failure, and more peace proposals followed. The Tenet plan and then the Mitchell Report came and went, and in 2002 the "road map" was devised. This called for phased and monitored peace moves between Israel and the Palestinians towards a settlement, supervised by the Quartet, and whose end would be a Palestinian state by 2005. But this also floundered.

A US-inspired international peace conference . . . is the latest attempt to revive the "peace process". It will bring Israelis, Palestinians and several Arab states together in Washington to endorse a "statement of principles" between Israeli Prime Minister Ehud Olmert and Palestinian President Mahmoud Abbas.

No negotiations are anticipated, since the parties are expected to have drawn up an agreement before the meeting.

The Israeli Plan to Stall Peace

The Arab states, which are reluctant to attend without an agreed agenda, are under US pressure to do so, but may not come. On the face of it, this initiative is more doomed than those before it. Olmert and Abbas are weak leaders with little popular support. Worse still, Abbas represents only one side of the split between Fatah, his party, and Hamas in Gaza. The latter is thus automatically excluded from any deal agreed to at the Washington meeting.

All these manoeuvrings are ostensibly about solving the conflict. But in reality, they substitute process for substance. Finding a solution to the Arab-Israeli conflict is not the problem. The parameters have been clear for decades: Israel's withdrawal from the 1967-occupied territories, the creation of a

Casualties of the Israeli-Palestinian Conflict from September 29, 2008 to August 31, 2008 by Location

	Occupied Territories			
	Gaza Strip	West Bank	Total	Israel
Palestinians killed by Israeli security forces	2970	1784	4754	69
Palestinians killed by Israeli civilians	4	41	45	3
Israeli civilians killed by Palestinians	39	197	236	490
Israeli security forces personnel killed by Palestinians	97	148	245	90
Foreign citizens killed by Palestinians	10	7	17	37
Foreign citizens killed by Israeli security forces	4	6	10	—
Palestinians killed by Palestinians	458	135	593	—

TAKEN FROM: B'tselem: The Israeli Information Center for Human Rights in the Occupied Territories, 2008.

Palestinian state with East Jerusalem as its capital, and the right of return of refugees. These are also the components of the 2002 Saudi plan and offer Israel full normalisation of relations with the Arab states in exchange.

The plan is in line with international law and has the support of the Western powers. Yet it has no chance of succeeding, nor has any other peace proposal not to Israel's liking.

And that is the nub of the problem. Israel, which ceaselessly professes its desire for peace, has never initiated a peace proposal of its own and has prevaricated when offered one. By postponing a settlement indefinitely, it has sought to gain time to colonise more Palestinian land, making that colonisation irreversible. This ploy has succeeded marvellously.

No Feasible Plan for Peace Exists

Today, Israel controls 46 per cent of the West Bank and the whole of Jerusalem. By building its barrier wall on West Bank territory, it has annexed the best Palestinian agricultural land and 80 per cent of its water to the Israeli side of the wall.

It dominates every aspect of Palestinian life, which it has transformed into a living hell through checkpoints and closures, arbitrary arrests, collective punishments, house demolitions and a vicious economic siege.

The dire effects of this regime have all been documented by the World Bank and various aid organisations. Yet this abuse of human rights, condemned by every international agency and legal body, even by some Israelis, continues unchecked.

A real peace process would have started here. By forcing Israel to accept that peace involves giving, not just taking, a proper settlement could begin to emerge. America, which could have made a difference, is hamstrung by its domestic subservience to the Israel lobby, and the EU [European Union] seems incapable of extricating itself from US policy.

So what will happen? Only three outcomes are possible: doing nothing (the current position), moving towards a two-state solution or creating one common state.

Leaving the status quo to fester will lead to more desperate acts of violence and more dangerous instability. Israel's colonisation has left the Palestinians with enclaves of land, separated by Jews-only roads and "security areas", cut off from each other and from Gaza, making the two-state solution as previously envisaged beyond reach.

Linking the Palestinian enclaves to Jordan in a confederation is under consideration as the only way to preserve a semblance of a Palestinian state, but it is far from agreed on.

That leaves the one-state option, rejected out of hand by Israel and its supporters, and viewed as hopelessly utopian by many others. And yet, it is the only one of the three that offers any hope of a lasting peace for Israelis and Palestinians and, by extension, everyone else.

But while power lies with Israel and its supporters, all solutions that Israel rejects will be pipe dreams.

"Hamas is now the government, and it is aware that it cannot govern and act as a terrorist force at the same time."

Peace Negotiations Are Possible Under Hamas Rule

Henry Siegman

Henry Siegman is a former senior fellow and director for the U.S./Middle East Project at the Council on Foreign Relations. In the following viewpoint, he argues that the Hamas-led government in Palestine, elected by the Palestinian people in 2006, will serve as a force for positive change and will help to move the peace process with Israel forward. While acknowledging the violent history of Hamas, Siegman highlights the positive platforms on which the party achieved its victory, such as the development of society and economy for Palestinians. Further, Siegman contends that Hamas's most recent ideological guidelines show the party to be moderate and seeking peace with Israel based on a two-state solution.

Note to readers: the following viewpoint is an excerpt from a longer version of the article presented.

Henry Siegman, "Hamas: The Last Chance for Peace?" *New York Review of Books*, vol. 53, April 27, 2006. Copyright © 2006 by NYREV, Inc. Reprinted with permission from The New York Review of Books.

As you read, consider the following questions:

1. What percentage of Palestinians believe that Hamas's priority should be the implementation of Islamic law, and what percentage support a two-state solution and peace deal with Israel, according to the poll cited by the author?

2. What is the "ideological trajectory" espoused by a senior member of Hamas's political committee?

3. According to Siegman, how do Hamas's new ideologies differ from their founding charter?

The rising tide of Muslim anger at the US and the West—as recorded by the Pew Poll and other opinion surveys—and the recent successes of political Islam have given many Israelis a newly urgent sense that they are under siege. Sever Plotzker, a well-known Israeli columnist, recently wrote in *Yedioth Ahronoth*, Israel's most widely circulated newspaper, that

> the Palestinian vote [which put Hamas into power] connects with the chilling phenomena taking place in the Arab world, whose resonant echoes penetrate every household in Israel.... Israel finds itself an inch away from an erupting volcano, on the frontlines of the "clash of civilization."

In Iraq, the Shiite parties defeated not only the Sunnis but also secular political parties; in Egypt, the Muslim Brotherhood's representation in the parliament increased five-fold; and in Palestine, legislative elections were swept by Hamas. The anti-Semitic rantings of Iran's President Mahmoud Ahmadinejad and his government's determination to develop nuclear weapons have only further exacerbated Israeli fears.

Israel is facing not only the threats of Hamas, an organization that has affirmed the right to violently resist Israel's occupation and has denied Israel's right to exist, but also the more general anger from the larger Muslim world toward the West. The two are often conflated, but it is a dangerously misleading conflation, for it gives a confused view of both the dangers and the opportunities created by Hamas's election victory, however meager the latter may appear to be.

The anger of the Muslim world toward the West is fueled by the humiliations of their Palestinian fellow Muslims who live under Israeli occupation; by what Muslims consider the theft of Palestine, land that is part of Dar al-Islam, the eternal domain of Muslims, in which the West has been complicit; by the war in Iraq and its aftermath; by the horrors that have occurred, and continue to occur, in US military prisons; and by the hypocrisies of America's plans to install democracy in various parts of the world. This hostility is seen as evidence of the religious and cultural confrontation between Islam and the Christian West that [American political scientist] Samuel Huntington has famously argued has become the new global fault line that has replaced the cold war. Paradoxically, the conflict between Israel and the Palestinians is the lesser of the two threats, because it is political rather than religious in character, and Palestinian society is among the most secular in the Arab world.

Even for Hamas, the national component of its struggle (ironically at odds with the "globalism" of traditional Islam that recognizes no national borders within the Domain of Islam) generally takes precedence over its religious imperatives when the two conflict. This is so not only because most Palestinians oppose Hamas's religious goals, particularly efforts to regulate their personal religious behavior, but more importantly because Hamas itself is as much a Palestinian national movement as it is a religious one.

In response to a call by Ayman al-Zawahiri, al-Qaeda's second in command, to Hamas to continue a violent jihad to recover every last "grain of soil from Palestine which was a Muslim land that was occupied by infidels," a Hamas official pointedly stated that "Hamas believes that Islam is completely different [from] the ideology of Mr. al-Zawahiri." He added,

"Our battle is against the Israeli occupation and our only concern is to restore our rights and serve our people." Now that Hamas has taken control of the Palestinian Legislative Council and the office of prime minister, the difference between Hamas and political Islam outside of Palestine defines what may be an opportunity that only a Hamas-led government may hold for Israel.

In the choice of candidates for the Palestinian Legislative Council, Hamas's "pragmatists," led by Ismail Haniyeh, the new prime minister, and Abed al-Aziz Duaik, the new speaker of the council, have visibly prevailed over those who are identified as Hamas's hard-liners. And many hard-liners themselves have adopted an increasingly moderate tone. Even hard-liners know that Hamas won the elections not because of their uncompromising ideology but because they ran on a moderate platform of clean government and better services. In a post-election opinion poll, only one percent of the respondents said that Hamas's priority should be to implement Islamic law in Palestine, while 73 percent said they still supported a peace deal with Israel and a two-state solution.

If Hamas's advocates of moderation were to prevail and a long-term coexistence were achieved between a Hamas-led Palestinian Authority and Israel, the implications of such an accommodation could be far-reaching indeed—for Israel's relations not only with the Palestinians but with the larger Muslim world as well. For Hamas's imprimatur on such an arrangement would provide Israel with an "insurance policy" of the sort that Fatah [the other major Palestinian political party] is not able to provide.

In his recent book, *Scars of War, Wounds of Peace*, Shlomo Ben Ami, a former foreign minister of Israel, writes of [former chairman of the Palestine Liberation Organization (PLO) Yasser] Arafat's passing from the political scene as a "tragedy" because he was "the only man whose signature on an agreement of compromise and reconciliation, which would include giving up unattainable dreams, could have been legitimate in the eyes of his people," and he took this legitimacy with him to the grave. The possibility of an Israeli-Palestinian agreement that enjoys comparable—indeed, perhaps even greater—legitimacy than Arafat could have conferred on it may have been revived by Hamas's entry into Palestinian political life.

Is such an optimistic outcome at all possible? At the least, it is too early to rule it out before the political and ideological trajectory of Hamas's new government can be discerned. The likely direction of that trajectory was recently described to me by a prominent senior member of Hamas's Political Committee in the following terms:

- Members of Hamas's political directorate do not preclude significant changes over time in their policies toward Israel and in their founding charter, including recognition of Israel, and even mutual minor border adjustments. Such changes depend on Israel's recognition of Palestinian rights. Hamas will settle for nothing less than full reciprocity.

- Hamas is not opposed to negotiations with Israel, provided negotiations are based on the provision that neither party may act unilaterally to change the situation that prevailed before the 1967 war, and that negotiations, when they are resumed, will take the pre-1967 border as their starting point.

- Hamas will not renounce its religious belief that Palestine is a *waqf*, or religions endowment, assigned by God to Muslims for all time. However, this theological belief does not preclude accommodation to temporal realities and international law, including Israel's statehood.

- Hamas is prepared to abide by a long-term *hudna*, or cease-fire, which would end all violence. Here again, complete reciprocity must prevail, and Israel must end all attacks on Palestinians. If Israel agrees to the cease-fire, Hamas will take responsibility for preventing and punishing Palestinian violations, whether committed by Islamic Jihad, the al-Aqsa Intifada, or its own people. Hamas understands that it cannot demand recognition as the legitimate government of Palestine if it is not prepared to enforce such a cease-fire, in the context of its responsibility for law and order.

- Hamas's first priority will be to revitalize Palestinian society by strengthening the rule of law, the independence of the judiciary, the separation of powers between various branches of government, and the professionalizing and accountability of the security services. It will aim to end corruption in government and implement new economic and social initiatives that are appropriate to the Palestinians' present circumstances. (My Hamas informant told me that well before the recent legislative elections, Hamas had commissioned teams of experts to prepare detailed plans for the economic and social recovery of Palestinian society; he said that the implementation of these plans would be Hamas's highest priority, but he did not discuss their content.)

- Hamas will not seek to impose standards of religious behavior and piety on the Palestinian population, such as the wearing of the veil or the *abaya*, although Hamas believes that certain standards of public modesty— but not of religious observance—should be followed by everyone.

These views are exceptional only in their comprehensiveness. Similar views have been expressed for some time by other Hamas moderates as well. Ismail Abu Shanab (assassinated by Israel) said that Hamas would halt its armed

Engaging the Politicians and the People

The state of the Palestinians and Israelis is intertwined. Their close contact under high pressure encompasses almost every dimension of social life, economically, geographically and even emotionally. An effective peacemaking process has to be a learning process. It is a joint journey, a difficult and a painful one, through which the two societies must learn how to accept each other and establish peaceful relations. This process has to be conducted on two levels that complete and support one another: that of the leadership (the political-elite model) and that of the people (the political-assembly model).

The political-elite model has been applied in almost infinite ways throughout the history of the Palestinian-Israeli conflict. Unfortunately, the focus was mostly directed toward searching for a solution to the conflict instead of building a comprehensive multi-dimensional process that would involve the public. Therefore any progression toward a peace agreement lacked the necessary social foundations for its implementation. Predictably almost every bold and creative peace enterprise has collapsed into violence. . . .

Sapir Handelman, "Two Complementary Views of Peacemaking: The Palestinian-Israeli Case," Middle East Policy, Fall 2008.

struggle if "the Israelis are willing to fully withdraw from the 1967 occupied territories and present a timetable for doing so."

The Hamas leader Mohammed Ghazal said last year [2005] that Hamas's charter is not the Koran. "Historically," he said, "we believe all Palestine belongs to Palestinians, but we're talking now about reality, about political solutions. . . . I don't think there will be a problem of negotiating with the Israelis." It is a sentiment echoed by Hasan Yousif, the Hamas leader in the West Bank who is now in an Israeli jail: "We have accepted the principle of accepting a Palestinian state within the 1967 borders."

More recently, and by far more importantly, Prime Minister Ismail Haniyeh said that not only did he approve a meeting between Palestinian President Mahmoud Abbas and [Israeli prime minister] Ehud Olmert but added that if Abbas brings back something that the Palestinian people approved, Hamas would change its positions. These sentiments are in striking contrast to the odiousness of Hamas's founding charter (of August 18, 1988), which relies on an extreme anti-Jewish reading of Islamic religious sources and on classical anti-Semitic defamations such as the Protocols of the Elders of Zion. Such hateful language was not entirely absent from PLO documents and statements in its pre-Oslo days, and one can find comparable demonization of Palestinians by some Jewish groups, including official Israeli political parties that advocate ethnic cleansing of all Palestinian residents of the West Bank. As noted by [former U.S. National Security Advisor and Secretary of State under President Richard Nixon] Henry Kissinger in a recent Op-Ed article, rejection and demonization are all too common in ethnic and political conflict, as is unexpected moderation by former extremists after they enter a political process and assume responsibility for the well-being of those who brought them to office.

The leaders of Israel's current government claim that no peace process is possible with a Hamas-led Palestinian government. But some of the best-informed observers of the Israeli-Palestinian conflict believe that no lasting peace between Israel and the Palestinians is possible *without* Hamas's participation. Nearly three years ago, well before anyone anticipated that

Hamas might be running the Palestinian Authority, Efraim Halevy, former head of the Mossad, Israel's CIA, wrote the following:

> Hamas constitutes about a fifth of Palestinian society. Because they are an active, engaged and aware group, they have more political weight. So anyone who thinks it's possible to ignore such a central element of Palestinian society is simply mistaken. Anyone who thinks that Hamas will one day evaporate is similarly mistaken. Abu Mazen [Mahmoud Abbas, the Palestinian prime minister] will not kill thousands of Palestinians in order to overcome the Islamic movements. In my view, then, the strategy vis-à-vis Hamas should be one of brutal force against its terrorist aspect, while at the same time signaling its political and religious leadership that if they take a moderate approach and enter the fabric of the Palestinian establishment, we will not view that as a negative development. I think that in the end there will be no way around Hamas being a partner in the Palestinian government. I believe that if that happens there is a chance that it will be domesticated. Its destructive force will be reduced.

Whatever one's reading of Hamas's intentions as it takes over the leadership of the Palestinian Authority, the notion that its sweeping electoral victory spells "the end of the peace process" is nonsense. The peace process died when Sharon was elected prime minister in 2000. More correctly, it was killed—with malice aforethought—by Sharon's "unilateralism" with which he implemented the disengagement from Gaza, which in turn provided cover for his continued unilateralism. That he was bringing off the disengagement against the wishes of the settlers helped to divert attention from his refusal to have any negotiations with the Palestinians.

Unilateralism continues to serve as the euphemism for Israeli policies that are expropriating half of what was to have been the state of Palestine, and are concentrating the Palestinian population, about to outnumber the Jewish population, in territorially disconnected Bantustans that make a mockery of the promise of an independent, sovereign, and viable Palestinian state made in the "road map" of 2003, which was put forward by the Quartet of the US, the EU, the UN, and Russia. . . .

Not only the European Union but the US government is on record that Israel's expropriations of large parts of the West Bank violate international law, the road map, and UN resolutions. It was not a Hamas spokesman but Condoleezza Rice [U.S. Secretary of State] who said, at a press conference following her recent meeting in Washington with Israel's Tzipi Livni, that "the United States position on [Israel's unilateralism] is very clear and remains the same. No one should try and unilaterally predetermine the outcome of a final status agreement. That's to be done at final status." Rice added that President Bush's letter to Prime Minister Ariel Sharon endorsing the need to take into consideration "new population centers" in the West Bank does not provide a license for anyone to "try and do that in a preemptive or predetermined way, because these are issues for negotiation at final status."

As to the issue of violence, Hamas declared a "calm" (*tahdiyah*) over a year ago, and largely observed it, despite Israel's resumption of targeted assassinations, which Israel had suspended in response to Hamas's initiative. Hamas has now offered to observe a long-term *hudna*, and is waiting for an Israeli reply.

Whether or not Hamas disbands its terrorist wing, the Izz al-Din al-Qassam Brigades, it is highly likely that a Hamas responsible for governance and the well-being of the Palestinian people will be a very different entity than a Hamas that acts in opposition to a Palestinian government. Hamas is now the government, and it is aware that it cannot govern and act as a terrorist force at the same time.

"The key question now is whether the Palestinians will have a secular future or an Islamist future."

Peace Negotiations Are Possible Under Fatah Rule

Dennis Ross

In the following viewpoint, Dennis Ross contends that the only way to solve the Israeli-Palestinian conflict is with the installment of a Fatah-led Palestinian government. Ross argues that the current Hamas-led government in Palestine continues to represent a radical faction of Islam that is unwilling to negotiate with Israel. Furthermore, he believes that Hamas represents a larger threat to the whole region due to its connections with Iran. He outlines the ways in which Fatah must remake itself to become a viable force against the current Hamas government, and he maintains that only under the leadership of Fatah—with help from the United States—will Palestine be able to enjoy a secular future. Dennis Ross is an author and Middle East expert who has been influential in helping to shape the Israeli-Palestinian peace process under presidents Bill Clinton and George H.W. Bush. Ross is most recently the author of Statecraft: And How to Restore America's Standing in the World.

As you read, consider the following questions:

1. What does Ross fear Hamas is attempting to do in building a unity government?

2. In what three ways does Ross believe Fatah must change in order to become a viable power?

3. According to the author, what is the United States' role in helping Fatah to regain power from Hamas?

It may be fashionable among some in Washington or even Tel Aviv to believe that it is time to talk to Hamas [the ruling party of the Palestinians]. But to the members of Fatah [the other substantial Palestinian political party] and the Palestinian independents in the West Bank with whom I have been meeting, it surely is not. What you hear from them is that Hamas is made up of killers; that they want to be part of a larger Islamist empire; that they are already trying to bring Iran to Gaza; and that the worst thing to do now is to reward Hamas with recognition.

Fatah Must Regain Power

For that reason, you also hear criticism of the Saudis who are pressing Mahmoud Abbas [president of the Palestinian National Authority] to reconcile with Hamas and forge a new national unity government. Indeed, I was struck by the almost unanimous sentiment that the reconciliation talks which both the Saudis and Egyptians are pushing—and Hamas leaders like Ismail Haniyeh favor—will not change Hamas's behavior. Instead, the story goes, Hamas will use them as a tactic to try to build its international acceptability. Worse, it would use a new national unity government to try to do in the West Bank what it has now done in Gaza.

Strong words, but is Fatah ready to compete? Can Fatah transform itself and connect again with the Palestinian public? Can its members reorganize themselves and build such a strong grassroots base that the balance of forces will change between Hamas and Fatah. (This competition might also affect the balance inside Hamas between those who are more programmatic and those who are most extreme). Hamas and within Hamas? Listen to Palestinians from different factions like Abu Kholi, a Palestinian Council member from Gaza, or Husayn Al-Sheikh, a member of the Tanzim from the West Bank, and you will hear that Fatah does not have a choice.

They will tell you that the Palestinian public is basically secular and wants a national, secular future. Hamas's position has grown within Palestinian society by default. The Palestinian public remains more alienated from Fatah than attracted to Hamas. But for Kholi, as-Sheikh, and others, all is not lost, and Fatah can regain its position in Palestinian society.

Ways to Make Fatah a Viable Power

To do so, several things are required. First, Fatah must have new leaders. If there was one phrase I heard more than any other, it was "Fatah must have new faces." No one meant that a simple veneer would suffice. Rather that the Palestinian public would never believe that Fatah had remade itself if the same people led Fatah. Interestingly, I found great support for Salam Fayyad, now the prime minister, foreign minister, and finance minister of the new emergency government of the Palestinian Authority (PA). He is not a member of Fatah, but his insistence on creating new institutions in the PA will inevitably build the credibility of the PA and, by extension, the credibility of Fatah.

Second, Fatah must be seen as delivering. What matters more than anything else is action and deeds, not only words. New faces in Fatah represent a starting point. But Fatah and the PA must be seen as active at the local level and being responsive socially and economically. Being responsive also means ending corruption and re-establishing not only the rule of law but a sense of security for Palestinians. It is interesting that Hamas is now trying to present itself in Gaza as restoring

Hamas and Hizballah Seek the Destruction of Israel

I am almost as old now as the State of Israel, and I sense that not in the past sixty years has there been a time when Israel has been so alone, vulnerable and threatened as it is today. Israel has always had enemies, of course. But as I have watched Hamas firing rockets at Sderot and now at Ashkelon [two Israeli cities], from a territory Israel has not occupied for two years, I think of Hizballah: During the summer of 2006 it amassed missiles at Israel's northern border at a time when Lebanon itself no longer had any territorial dispute with Israel (save the ambiguous, minute and artificial Shebaa Farms affair). In other words, here we have two adversaries of Israel, Hamas and Hizballah, who no longer have claims that are intelligible within the classical logic of political conflict. Today, at least, the demands of the Palestinians may be seen as exaggerated and unrealistic, but at least there are demands. Hamas and Hizballah demand nothing from Israel, except that it be annihilated. Their actions are not based on strategy but on a brutal and naked hatred, one that no negotiation or concession can slake.

Bernard-Henri Lévy, "The Task of the Jews,"
The American Interest, *September-October 2008.*

law and order. Fayyad is clearly trying to do the same thing in the West Bank. I saw an unprecedented number of heavily armed security forces in uniform on the ground in Ramallah. And Fayyad told me that this is deliberate: He is trying to establish a presence in each city to show that the PA is re-establishing order. Will the armed militias and the Al Aqsa

Martyrs' Brigades disarm or be incorporated in a disciplined way into the security forces? That remains a huge question, but Fayyad, at least, is trying to make the decree on disarming something other than an empty promise. Time will tell whether he can deliver on what he is trying to do, but I found much support for his efforts among some of the Tanzim that I met.

Third, there does need to be a sense of possibility about peace with Israel. A process, negotiations, dialogue, and the promise of changes on the ground will count for a lot. Ironically, I did not find the Palestinians I spoke with—and the number is now over 40 in my two visits here in the last six weeks—wanting to raise false expectations. No one expects an immediate breakthrough and resolution of the permanent status issues. Of course, that would be desirable. But what I saw was a desire for real, not illusionary changes. Changes that showed that day-to-day life, economically and practically in terms of mobility, would be transformed. Such changes would make permanent status negotiations more believable. Permanent status disconnected from the day-to-day realities will have no credibility. Palestinians would ask me, "If I cannot get from Nablus to Jenin, am I supposed to believe that I will have a state with an East Jerusalem capital?" That is why security and any political process are inevitably tied together.

Credibility Comes from the United States

All this has lessons for American statecraft now. We must keep our eye on the essential objective. The key question now is whether the Palestinians will have a secular future or an Islamist future. Our stake in a national, secular future for the Palestinians is very clear. Without that, there will be no prospect of peace, and Islamists will control the most evocative issue in the region. We should quietly be making that point with the Saudis. Pushing now for a national unity government will only strengthen Hamas, and Hamas's long-term success will mean that Iran will be able to use the Palestinian grievance and ongoing conflict as an instrument to keep the Saudis and others on the defensive.

Beyond this, our essential challenge is going to be how to ensure that Fatah succeeds. While many in Fatah understand the stakes and what is necessary, the call for new faces in Fatah means that the old faces have to be willing to step aside. There are no signs that they are ready to do so. Is Abbas ready to push them? It will go against his very nature to do so. But there is no alternative, and our role and new Middle East envoy Tony Blair's role will require constant pushing in this regard. But we can't just push. We must also deliver real resources. If there was one other refrain I heard from Palestinians, it was "Don't embrace Abbas and Fayyad unless you are also going to deliver real goods to them." Supporting them with great words will only destroy their credibility if we do not also deliver noticeable assistance that will at least improve the economic situation on the ground.

Results on the ground and real hopes will help Fatah. Secretary of State Condoleezza Rice would do well to keep this in mind. A credible negotiating process is one thing; a symbolic event like an international conference where only hard-line speeches are given that highlight how little prospect of agreement there is, and where there is no practical follow-up, is another. Palestinians are not looking for symbols now. They know the difference between symbols and reality. Let's hope the Bush administration does as well.

> *"The Palestinian Authority should be held accountable for all violence coming from its territories, and Israelis should be compensated by the Palestinian Authority for all acts of terrorism."*

Palestine Must Abandon Terrorism and Accept Israel's Legitimacy if Peace Is to Be Achieved

Newt Gingrich

Former Republican congressman Newt Gingrich served as speaker of the U.S. House of Representatives from 1995 to 1999. In the following viewpoint, he concedes that there is some use to diplomatic meetings between Israelis and Palestinians in brokering a peace agreement, but he maintains that all diplomatic measures are hollow and useless in creating a lasting peace if the Palestinian government does not take responsibility for the actions of terrorists who commit violence on behalf of their country. Gingrich calls on the leaders of the Palestinians to put a halt to all acts of terrorism and recognize Israel as a state. He states that only when Palestinian leadership begins to take responsibility for

Newt Gingrich, "Defeat of Terror, Not Roadmap Diplomacy, Will Bring Peace," *Middle East Quarterly*, Summer 2005. Copyright © 2005 The Middle East Forum. Reproduced by permission.

the actions of its citizens will the peace process move forward and bring permanent stability to the region.

As you read, consider the following questions:

1. According to Gingrich, what two threats does Israel face if the war between Israelis and Palestinians continues?
2. Who does the author believe should take responsibility for the burden of violence and preventing terrorism?
3. What does the "new set of metrics for success," proposed by the author, entail?

Many observers hold that the death of former Palestinian leader Yasir Arafat and the subsequent election of Mahmoud Abbas to lead the Palestinian Authority have created a window of opportunity for the U.S. government to set a course for a lasting peace between Israel and the Palestinian people. For the Palestinians, this should mean a democratic Palestinian state under the rule of law and the right to pursue health, prosperity, and freedom. For Israel, this should mean national security and peace. For the White House, there are both practical and moral imperatives to encourage the Israeli and Palestinian people to live together. Regional Middle East peace and security will translate into an ability in Washington to devote attention and resources to other areas of increasing strategic concern, such as the growing dangers from a nuclear-armed North Korea and the unabated poverty and disease in sub-Saharan Africa. Strategically, a protracted conflict will continue to destabilize the Middle East and complicate our relations with Europe. It is to Washington's disadvantage to have the Israeli-Palestinian conflict continue for another generation.

Threats to Israel

Israelis will face two existential threats if the war continues: first, there is a danger of growing isolation from the rest of the world as Israel's dominant military capabilities make it look like a bully and oppressor. Indeed, Israel has been losing sympathy around the world since 1982 when Ariel Sharon, then minister of defense, took the Israeli army into Beirut. For the last twenty years, the rhetoric against Israel in Europe and on the American left has grown stronger. Another generation of military reprisals, no matter how legitimate in terms of responding to terrorist killings of innocent people, may leave Israel dangerously isolated. This trend is complicated both by the increasing Muslim population in Western Europe and the European sympathy for the plight of the Palestinian people, which is increasingly leading to an acceptance of the view that terrorism is a legitimate response to the dominance of the Israeli military. European officials, trying to placate their new residents, find it easy to posit an anti-Israel stance for domestic consumption, thus unintentionally reinforcing growing anti-Semitic views inside their countries.

Second, there is the real danger that those who are determined to destroy Israel will acquire weapons of mass destruction. Such weapons are already in the hands of North Korea and Pakistan—two countries hostile to Israel's existence. The potential for these weapons to find their way into neighboring nations is troubling, in particular because Syria, which has repeatedly failed to apprehend known terrorists from within its borders, possesses a large number of chemical warheads. Compounding the threat is Iran, believed by many countries to be secretly developing nuclear weapons. Another generation of continuing hatred and violence could culminate in a devastating attack with horrifying casualties. Israel simply does not have the strategic depth or the ability to disperse its population sufficiently to survive a first strike of significant magnitude.

Israel's desire for safety provides a powerful incentive to seek a constructive resolution to the historic conflict. However, for the vast majority of Palestinians, there is an equally powerful imperative for dramatically improving their quality of life.

Reforming the Palestinian Government

The Palestinians entered their war with Israel as a relatively wealthy, educated, and cosmopolitan people. They were in some ways among the most international and most advanced people in the Arab world. The long conflict has destroyed their hopes for a better future, left them without a viable economy, and for too long, left them without responsible leadership.

The Arab emphasis on a rigidly defined "right of return" for Palestinians—something no Arab government would grant the equally large number of Jews who migrated from Arab countries to Israel—has been an excuse to keep Palestinian refugees in United Nations camps without property, prosperity, or dignity.

Because the Palestinian Authority's underlying system of intimidation, terrorist support, and kleptocracy [making government leaders wealthy at the expense of the citizens of the government] has been an impediment to the institutional reforms necessary to enforce the rule of law within the Palestinian-controlled territories, it is incumbent upon Abbas to demonstrate that he is serious about securing a lasting peace and improving the lives of the Palestinian people by controlling both armed terrorists and the local criminals who have for too long preyed on their own compatriots.

As a first step, Abbas must advance substantive government reform by replacing old dominant factions within the Palestinian Authority with an honest, responsible, transparent, and accountable system intolerant of terrorism and willing to live in peace with Israel. Abbas, like his predecessor, has not controlled the terrorist groups that pursue agendas irreconcilable with peace. That, however, does not permit Abbas to cease trying, nor should it let some Europeans continue to support blindly the dictatorial wing of Palestinian society. The ability of a Palestinian minority to deny the opportunity for the Palestinian people to live in peace, prosperity, and freedom should not be tolerated. Nor should Palestinian officials sympathetic to the radical minority be allowed to stay in power. Abbas should dismiss those who have sacrificed and would continue to sacrifice their people's future for their own enrichment. . . .

Diplomacy Was Misused in the Past

Focusing only on diplomacy as the path to success is wrong.

Diplomacy is important and has a vital role to play, but its function must be different than the Oslo process and the roadmap suggest. The focus on Israeli-Palestinian diplomacy cannot work when one side has a leadership that does not deliver on its word. The State Department may wish to give Abbas the benefit of the doubt. As with Arafat, Abbas says the right things in English to the Western press, but his commitment is not yet tested. So far, there is little evidence that the recognized faction has any more interest in dealing with its terrorist factions than it did under Arafat's leadership. It has shown some will, however, to cease making its priority the enrichment of the Palestinian oligarchy [government where only a few people hold all the power]. Hopefully, the new Palestinian leadership will show at least some desire to crackdown on terrorist groups.

At this moment, however, the Palestinian Authority continues to use threats of terrorism as a negotiating tool. As recently as February 2005, Palestinian Authority officials warned that without the release of thousands of prisoners, an upcoming Palestinian-Israeli summit would not succeed. "If Israeli intransigence on this issue continues, the summit will fail," said Minister of Communications Azzam al-Ahmed. "If the prisoners aren't released, we will return to the cycle of violence."

Hamas, too, maintained its terrorist rhetoric regardless of diplomacy between U.S. officials and the Palestinian Authority. Abdel Aziz Rantisi, the late Hamas spokesman, summed up the group's position, saying, "I am telling Sharon and all the Israeli murderers, you don't have any security unless you leave the country. There will be no single Jew in Palestine. We will fight them with all the power that we have." As [former mayor of New York] Ed Koch has pointed out, Rantisi's vision of a future without Jews is no different from Adolf Hitler's intent on making Europe *Judenrein* [Nazi term meaning an area without a Jewish presence]. It is impossible to engage diplomatically with those who espouse irreconcilable positions.

Shifting the Burden of Violence

Israel has spent the last fifty-seven years trying to protect itself within a system in which every Israeli action is described as a provocation and every Israeli retaliation is described as disproportionate and inappropriate. . . .

The burden of the resulting violence should be upon those who commit terrorism. When a neighborhood shelters terrorists, it should not be surprised at a violent response. When a rocket or mortar is fired from a neighborhood, people should expect retaliatory fire. When someone advocates killing Israelis, they should expect to be killed by those they plan to kill.

The burden for preventing terrorism should rest on the Palestinian Authority. Western governments should not bestow the privileges of governance without its responsibilities. The Palestinian Authority should be held accountable for all violence coming from its territories, and Israelis should be compensated by the Palestinian Authority for all acts of terrorism. The rules of normal international behavior should apply to both sides. . . .

Remapping the Road to Peace

The new strategy should be based on new premises, carried out by new organizational relationships, and focus on a new set of metrics for success. First, both Western governments and their Arab allies should recognize that there is a real war underway between a minority of the Palestinians and the Israelis. This minority of Palestinians has one goal: to destroy Israel. It is impossible to negotiate with this group, and it is equally impossible for the Israelis to engage in rounds of diplomacy when their women and children are being brutally murdered in an ongoing dance of death and destruction.

Second, the goal must be to establish safety for the Israeli people. It is the duty of a government to protect its own citizens.

Third, it is important to recognize that the vast, but intimidated, majority of the Palestinian people would like to live in safety, health, prosperity, and freedom. Most Palestinians do not want their children living in war torn neighborhoods surrounded by poverty and devastation. They do not want to live their lives under the heel of a corrupt, brutal, and incompetent dictatorship.

Fourth, protecting Israel and developing a peaceful Palestinian leadership has to precede any lasting diplomatic solution. Instead of focusing on diplomacy, the White House and State Department should develop two parallel tracks, one for helping Israel defend itself and the other for helping the Palestinian people develop a better future.

The president should state unambiguously that only when there is a stable, peaceful West Bank and Gaza and when Israelis are living in a safe country with no casualties, can the two sides negotiate complex issues such as the status of Jerusalem. Such a policy would put the burden on the Palestinian leadership to create the environment that would allow them to come to the negotiating table.

The intelligence community, police, military, economists, business and medical communities all matter more than the bilateral diplomatic discourse. Only when these elements have succeeded, will it be time once again to call on the Israeli and Palestinian diplomats. . . .

Putting the Palestinian People First

Israel can only find peace when Israel has a partner capable of enforcing the peace. The fanciest diplomatic agreements are of no value if those who seek violence can defeat and intimidate those who seek peace. The key first step toward a lasting peace is not at the negotiating table, but inside Palestinian society.

The Palestinian leadership should replicate the same hard choices that the Irish Free State made in 1922 when it reached the conclusion that it had to defeat the Irish Republican Army if it was ever going to have a stable, independent Ireland. The Irish case is instructive. While the power of the British Empire had been inadequate to defeat the Irish Republican Army over a six-year period (1916–1922), the new Irish Free State won the civil war in a few months.

The Irish Free State's leadership put its people first. The Palestinian leadership has until now shown no inclination to do likewise. It remains impossible to establish an independent Palestine for three reasons. First, Palestinian terrorists are prepared to kill those who advocate compromise. Those who favor a better future are too disorganized, too timid, and too untrained to defeat the forces of terrorism. Second, the Palestinian Authority's corrupt machine has viewed any real reforms as a threat to its survival and threatens with violence any true reformers. Lastly, there has been no systematic effort from the outside to identify, organize, train, finance, and equip a responsible wing of the Palestinian people in opposition to terrorists whether they are in Hamas's camp or in the Palestinian Authority's.

For the Palestinians to move forward, the matrix for their government's success should be its ability to bring security, health, prosperity, and freedom for its people. Washington should identify and work with responsible Palestinians who share these goals. By insisting that resources and support will go only to those Palestinians who work actively for an accountable, democratic Palestinian government willing to live in peace with Israel, the White House and State Department can establish a basis on which to build a movement and an accountable government.

Pressure from the West

The State Department should strongly urge the European Union and the United Nations [U.N.] to insist on transparency and accountability in money being sent into the Palestinian territories. The multi-billion dollar corruption being unearthed in the U.N.'s Oil-for-Food program in Iraq gives Washington the high ground to insist that the Palestinian oligarchs not be allowed to steal from their people and from donors, as Saddam [Hussein, former president of Iraq] long did. To this aim, there should be an outside independent audit of past expenditures by the United Nations in the camps that its Refugee Works Administration operates. The Palestinian people should expect a full accounting for the money that has been stolen. Forensic investigators should track down all the assets of a lifetime of theft and insist that it be paid back to the Palestinian people.

Congress should establish a program of economic aid for the Palestinian people to match the aid the U.S. government provides Israel. Palestinian aid would be largely economic and for policing while security concerns necessitate that Israel receive a far higher military component. The goal of U.S. aid should be to bring education, jobs, and health care to the Palestinians, not to line the pockets of its leadership. The Bush administration should challenge the Europeans and Arab countries to join in this program.

Congress might also pass a tax credit for businesses and individuals willing to invest in Israeli-Palestinian joint ventures and to subsidize the creation of Palestinian free trade and free investment zones.

It is important not only that Western democracies help the Palestinian leadership develop the infrastructure of a respon-

Rewarding Palestinian Weakness on Terror

Last November's [2007] Annapolis Conference, conceived by Secretary of State Condoleezza Rice to culminate in a final status agreement by the end of 2008, could have been seen as a step forward [in the Israel-Palestine peace process]. Although recently expectations have been scaled back considerably ... it was the first time that Israelis and Palestinians gathered around an international conference table based on the explicit understanding that the resolution of the conflict between them involved two states living side-by-side in peace. ...

But Annapolis also suppressed harsh realities. Most fundamental, in achieving a final status agreement, no Palestinian leader can settle for anything less than full Palestinian sovereignty in most of the West Bank, while no Israeli leader can agree to full Palestinian sovereignty until the terrorist cells exposing the greater Tel Aviv area—Israel's commercial and cultural hub and home to half the country's population—to suicide bombers and Katyusha and Kassam rockets have been rooted out. Moreover, returning to the negotiating table at Annapolis meant the abandonment by the Bush administration and Israel of their clearly declared position that progress toward peace depended on the Palestinians' halting terrorism. The result was to reward Palestinian weakness and lack of resolve in combating the terrorists among them—if not Palestinian terror altogether. ...

Peter Berkowitz, "Peaceless,"
Policy Review, *August-September 2008.*

sible state, but also that the West stands united in pressuring those countries which continue to support Palestinian terrorism. Both the Europeans and Washington should make it clear that they regard this as an act of hostility to them and no longer acceptable under any circumstance.

Resources in and Around Gaza

As the Israeli economy continues to develop into one of the world's most important high technology centers, its demand for labor is an enormous opportunity to enrich Palestinians while also enriching Israelis. As Palestinian entrepreneurs learn to work with Israeli entrepreneurs in creating jobs and wealth for both people, the opportunity is enormous for the Palestinians to develop the highest income among the non-oil economies of the Middle East.

Palestinian population density and the small size of its territory need not be impediments to a productive future. Hong Kong and Singapore are both more crowded than Gaza, but both are richer than Gaza by enormous margins. Gaza has the benefit of proximity to both Israel's high-technology economy and all the wealth of Europe. There is no inherent reason the people of Gaza could not have a terrific future of opportunity and prosperity.

Gaza even has great potential for tourism. Its beaches are far warmer than the beaches of Italy. There is no reason they should be less profitable. The potential for religious tourism in the West Bank is obvious. Bethlehem, Hebron, and Jericho have a historic and tourist interest to billions of Asians whose rising incomes have bolstered their interest in travel. As terrorists are defeated and the West Bank becomes safe, there is every reason to believe the tourist industry could rebound and bring substantial prosperity to the area. Such economic opportunities could convince Palestinian youth to seek a better future instead of violent death.

Encouraging Investment in Palestine

Fulfillment of these goals will require that the Palestinian education system be overhauled to make it pro-jobs and pro-economic productivity and to eliminate anti-Israel propaganda from the school system. No state-supported newspaper, radio or television stations should engage in anti-Israeli incitement. Monitoring should be intense, and complaints be immediate and with real financial consequence if the agreement is not maintained.

The West is not operating in a vacuum. Many states wish to see a Palestinian democracy fail. They will seek to impose a radical agenda by means of self-described humanitarian organizations. The West should develop secular systems of humanitarian aid for impoverished and ill Palestinians that outperform those support systems run by terrorist organizations. Unfortunately, most Western nongovernmental organizations do not fit the bill. Many have proved themselves to be committed more toward leftist politics than they are to peace.

The Palestinians should be equally responsible for their future. One of the real tests of the new, more responsible Palestinian system will be the ability to assure fellow Palestinians from abroad that they are personally safe and that their money is safe if they want to invest in their ancestral lands and help create wealth. The Palestinian diaspora has been remarkably successful in business. It can help modernize and make prosperous the Palestinian people, just as many Iraqi businessmen have chosen since Iraq's liberation to invest in their own homeland. There is great wealth and, even more important, great knowledge and great contacts among the Palestinian expatriates. If they can be convinced to help their fellow Palestinians prosper as Jews across the world have been doing for Israel since 1948, then the prospects of creating a truly prosperous Gaza and West Bank will increase dramatically. Arafat's failure to engage the great talents of Palestinians overseas is a reflection of the general failure.

Defeating Terror to Gain Prosperity

Those Palestinians whose hatred of Israel trumps their desire to win a better future for the next generation may wish to ignite a civil war against the forces of Palestinian tolerance and democracy. No one should underestimate how violent and how bitter this civil war could be. Mao Zedong [former leader of the Communist Party of China] wrote that all power comes out of the end of a rifle. He also wrote that one man with a rifle can control 100 villagers without a weapon. The forces of terrorism have relied on the power of the violent to dominate the tolerant. The U.S. government must strengthen the responsible elements of society so they can defeat the haters and the killers.

Rather than shrink from responsibility, Washington should step forward to defend freedom and democracy. We have done this before, not only helping the Philippines secretary of national defense Ramon Magsaysay defeat the Communist Hukbalahap in the Philippines in the late 1940s but also working together with Great Britain to help anti-Communists defeat the Communist guerrillas in Greece in the wake of World War II. U.S. aid allowed the government of El Salvador to win a full-blown civil war in the 1980s. There are a number of other occasions where intervention on the side of a responsible party defeated terrorists.

In effect, Washington would be offering the Palestinian people a straight proposition: if you defeat terrorism and accept Israel as a neighbor, we can invest enough resources to help you become prosperous and create a safe, free country in which people have a good future.

"The one-state solution . . . neither de-stroys the Jewish character of the Holy Land nor negates the Jewish historical and religious attachment."

Israelis and Palestinians Should Share One Democratic State

Michael Tarazi

A legal advisor to the Palestine Liberation Organization (PLO), Michael Tarazi argues in the following viewpoint that a one-state solution is the only choice for peace between Israelis and Palestinians. Tarazi states that Israel and Palestine are too inter-mingled to separate into geographically distinct states. He notes that both peoples already share state sponsored infrastructure, such as highways and electricity grids, and other ties, making Is-rael and Palestine effectively one state. However, Tarazi states that in order for both peoples to have peace and prosperity, Is-raelis must begin treating Palestinians as equals in their shared state.

As you read, consider the following questions:

1. What percentage of Palestinians support a one-state so-lution, according to polls cited by the author?

2. What example does Tarazi give to show the second-class citizen situation which the 3.5 million Palestinians must abide?

3. To which struggle for equality does the author compare the current situation in Israel and does this comparison make him hopeful?

Israel's untenable policy in the Middle East was more obvious than usual . . . , as the Israeli Army made repeated incursions into Gaza [in September 2004], killing dozens of Palestinians in the deadliest attacks in more than two years, even as [former] Prime Minister Ariel Sharon reiterated his plans to withdraw from the territory. Israel's overall strategy toward the Palestinians is ultimately self-defeating: it wants Palestinian land but not the Palestinians who live on that land.

The Israeli Democratic Threat

As Christians and Muslims, the millions of Palestinians under occupation are not welcome in the Jewish state. Many Palestinians are now convinced that Israeli support for a Palestinian state is motivated not by a hope for reconciliation, but by a desire to segregate non-Jews while taking as much of their land and resources as possible. They are increasingly questioning the most commonly accepted solution to the Palestinian-Israeli conflict—"two states living side by side in peace and security," in the words of President [George W.] Bush—and are being forced to consider a one-state solution.

To Palestinians, the strategy behind Israel's two-state solution is clear. More than 400,000 Israelis live illegally in more than 150 colonies, many of which are atop Palestinian water sources. Mr. Sharon is prepared to evacuate settlers from Gaza—but only in exchange for expanding settlements in the West Bank. And Israel is building a barrier wall not on its land but rather inside occupied Palestinian territory. The wall's route maximizes the amount of Palestinian farmland and water on one side and the number of Palestinians on the other.

Yet while Israelis try to allay a demographic threat, they are creating a democratic threat. After years of negotiations, coupled with incessant building of settlements and now the construction of the wall, Palestinians finally understand that Israel is offering "independence" on a reservation stripped of water and arable soil, economically dependent on Israel and even lacking the right to self-defense.

The Middle Eastern Apartheid

As a result, many Palestinians are contemplating whether the quest for equal statehood should now be superseded by a struggle for equal citizenship. In other words, a one-state solution in which citizens of all faiths and ethnicities live together as equals. Recent polls indicate that a quarter of Palestinians favor the secular one-state solution—a surprisingly high number given that it is not officially advocated by any senior Palestinian leader.

Support for one state is hardly a radical idea; it is simply the recognition of the uncomfortable reality that Israel and the occupied Palestinian territories already function as a single state. They share the same aquifers, the same highway network, the same electricity grid and the same international borders. There are no road signs reading "Welcome to Occupied Territory" when one drives into East Jerusalem. Some government maps of Israel do not delineate Israel's 1967 pre-occupation border. Settlers in the occupied West Bank (including East Jerusalem) are interspersed among Palestinian towns and now constitute nearly a fifth of the population. In the words of one Palestinian farmer, you can't unscramble an egg.

But in this de facto state, 3.5 million Palestinian Christians and Muslims are denied the same political and civil rights as

Historical Roots of the Israeli-Palestinian Conflict

For 60 years, both the Israelis and the Palestinians have used the past to illuminate the present and confer legitimacy on their nations' respective founding myths. Of course, Zionists and Palestinian nationalists were not the first to embellish the stories of their nations' births or make excuses for their tragedies. Throughout history, nations have been born in blood and frequently in sin. This is why, as the French philosopher Ernest Renan wrote, they tend to lie about their pasts.

The birth of the state of Israel in 1948 has long been the subject of self-congratulatory historiography by the victorious side and grievance-filled accounts by disinherited Palestinians. To the Israelis, the 1948 war was a desperate fight for survival that was settled by an almost miraculous victory. In the Arab world, accounts of the war tend to advance conspiracy theories and attempt to shift the blame for the Arabs' defeat. In both cases, the writing of history has been part of an uncritical nationalist quest for legitimacy.

Refusing to admit that the noble Jewish dream of statehood was stained by the sins of Israel's birth and eager to deny the centrality of the Palestinian problem to the wider conflict in the Middle East, the Israelis have preferred to dwell on their struggle for independence against the supposedly superior invading Arab armies. . . .

Shlomo Ben-Ami, "A War to Start All Wars,"
Foreign Affairs, *September-October 2008.*

Jews. These Palestinians must drive on separate roads, in cars bearing distinctive license plates, and only to and from designated Palestinian areas. It is illegal for a Palestinian to drive a car with an Israeli license plate. These Palestinians, as non-Jews, neither qualify for Israeli citizenship nor have the right to vote in Israeli elections.

In South Africa, such an allocation of rights and privileges based on ethnic or religious affiliation was called apartheid. In Israel, it is called the Middle East's only democracy.

The Struggle for Equality

Most Israelis recoil at the thought of giving Palestinians equal rights, understandably fearing that a possible Palestinian majority will treat Jews the way Jews have treated Palestinians. They fear the destruction of the never-defined "Jewish state." The one-state solution, however, neither destroys the Jewish character of the Holy Land nor negates the Jewish historical and religious attachment (although it would destroy the superior status of Jews in that state). Rather, it affirms that the Holy Land has an equal Christian and Muslim character.

For those who believe in equality, this is a good thing. In theory, Zionism is the movement of Jewish national liberation. In practice, it has been a movement of Jewish supremacy. It is this domination of one ethnic or religious group over another that must be defeated before we can meaningfully speak of a new era of peace; neither Jews nor Muslims nor Christians have a unique claim on this sacred land.

The struggle for Palestinian equality will not be easy. Power is never voluntarily shared by those who wield it. Palestinians will have to capture the world's imagination, organize the international community and refuse to be seduced into negotiating for their rights.

But the struggle against South African apartheid proves the battle can be won. The only question is how long it will take, and how much all sides will have to suffer, before Israeli

Jews can view Palestinian Christians and Muslims not as demographic threats but as fellow citizens.

Periodical Bibliography

The following articles have been selected to supplement the diverse views presented in this chapter.

Fouad Ajami
"A Reality Check as Israel Turns 60," *U.S. News & World Report*, May 19, 2008.

Kay Argyll
"Making Sense of the Arab-Israel Nightmare," *Washington Report on Middle East Affairs*, September-October 2008.

Ed Blanche
"West Bank Land Grab," *Middle East*, June 2008.

Steve Burgess
"Let My People Flow," *Maclean's*, July 28, 2008.

CQ Researcher
"Is U.S. Support for Israel the Main Obstacle to Peace in the Middle East?" October 27, 2006.

Neve Gordon
"Nowadays Israelis and Palestinians Lead Very Separate Lives," *National Catholic Reporter*, August 8, 2008.

Samah Jabr
"Denying the Palestinian Nakba: Sixty Years Is Enough," *Washington Report on Middle East Affairs*, April 2008.

Morton A. Kaplan
"Why Plans for a Two-State Solution in the Middle East Have Failed," *International Journal on World Peace*, March 2008.

Isabel Kershner
"Israel Aids Palestinians with Arms," *New York Times*, September 6, 2008.

Tim McGirk
"The Long View," *Time*, May 19, 2008.

Kevin Peraino and Joana Chen
"The Trouble with Silence," *Newsweek*, March 17, 2008.

Michael Petrou
"Why Israel Can't Survive," *Maclean's*, May 5, 2008.

CHAPTER 3

Is Iran a Threat to the United States and Its Allies?

Chapter Preface

In March 2008, Vice President Dick Cheney accused the government of Iran of seeking to enrich uranium stores to weapons-grade levels, thus progressing toward the construction of a nuclear warhead. In his 2008 State of the Union address, President George W. Bush cast similar warnings, claiming, "Tehran is . . . developing ballistic missiles of increasing range, and continues to develop its capability to enrich uranium, which could be used to create a nuclear weapon." Such fears of a nuclear Iran have prompted many to insist that America take action to prevent Tehran from acquiring warheads and missiles that could reach Israel, China, or Russia and lead to a destabilization of the region.

Despite the call to arms, there has been no definitive proof that Iran's nuclear ambitions are hostile. Iran has, for years, claimed that its enrichment of uranium is part of a civilian nuclear energy program. The International Atomic Energy Agency, which oversees Iran's nuclear progress, seems to support this view, acknowledging that Iran's enrichment efforts have yielded only the type of low-grade uranium needed to fuel its newly constructed nuclear power reactor at Bushehr. A 2007 U.S. intelligence report also concluded that Iran ceased its nuclear weapons program in 2003 due to international pressures. That report estimated that at Iran's reduced pace of enrichment, it could not acquire enough weapons-grade uranium until sometime between 2010 and 2015.

Such estimates do not calm many critics. Israeli government officials are particularly worried given that Iran's Shahab missiles have sufficient range to reach the Mediterranean Sea. Shaul Mofaz, Isael's transportation minister and former defense minister, told a conference of Jewish organizations in New York that "If we cannot derail the Iranian train from the tracks, we are on the verge of a nuclear era that will totally al-ter the regional reality." To "derail" Iran, the Israeli government is suggesting that it may take military action against Iran's nuclear sites to at least delay its supposed nuclear schedule. Israel has sought support from the United States for its proposed actions, but so far, official approval has not been given.

In the following chapter, two authors debate the pros and cons of launching attacks against Iran to limit the country's nuclear ambitions. They are among several commentators in the chapter who discuss how threatening a presence Iran is in the Middle East and how best to defuse the tense situation that has developed around its potential acquisition of weapons of mass destruction.

> "The U.S. Intelligence Community be-
> lieves Iran could have a nuclear weapon
> sometime in the beginning to the
> middle of the next decade."

Iran Is a Threat to the United States and Its Allies

U.S. House of Representatives Permanent Select Committee on Intelligence

In the following viewpoint, the U.S. House of Representatives Permanent Select Committee on Intelligence offers evidence that Iran is building nuclear weapons, enhancing its chemical and biological weapons capabilities, and improving its ballistic missile programs. The House committee fears that, with such destructive power, Iran could point weapons of mass destruction (WMD) at a variety of targets in the region and beyond. Coupled with Tehran's support of terrorism, the House committee warns that Iran's WMD achievements are a direct threat to the United States, its allies, and peace in the Middle East. The House Permanent Select Committee on Intelligence oversees the nation's intelligence networks. The subcommittee that drafted this viewpoint was chaired by Mike Rogers, a Republican from Michigan.

U.S. House of Representatives Permanent Select Committee on Intelligence, *Recognizing Iran as a Strategic Threat: An Intelligence Challenge for the United States.* Washington, DC: U.S. House of Representatives Permanent Select Committee on Intelligence, 2006.

As you read, consider the following questions:

1. According to the committee, about how many nuclear warheads could Iran make if it enriched its supposed 85-ton stock of uranium hexafluoride?

2. As stated in the committee report, why does the U.S. Department of State believe that Iran is in violation of its Chemical Weapon Convention obligations?

3. How is Iran actively working against U.S. interests in Iraq, in the House committee's view?

Iran poses a threat to the United States and its allies due to its sponsorship of terror, probable pursuit of weapons of mass destruction, and support for the insurgency in Iraq. The profile of the Iranian threat has increased ... due to the election of President Mahmoud Ahmadinejad, who has made public threats against the United States and Israel, the continuation of Iranian nuclear weapons research, and the recent attacks by Hezbollah, an Iranian terrorist proxy, against Israel. Iran has provided Hezbollah with financial support and weapons, including the thousands of rockets Hezbollah fired against Israel in July and August 2006. Iran thus bears significant responsibility for the recent violence in Israel and Lebanon.

Iran's efforts since December 2005 to resume enrichment of uranium, in defiance of the international community, Tehran's willingness to endure international condemnation, isolation, and economic disruptions in order to carry out nuclear activities covertly indicates Iran is developing nuclear weapons. . . .

Iran's Nuclear Weapons Program

Two decades ago, Iran embarked on a secret program to acquire the capability to produce weapons—grade nuclear material. Iran has developed an extensive infrastructure, from laboratories to industrial facilities, to support its research for nuclear weapons. Producing fissile material is a complicated process and Tehran faces several key obstacles to acquiring a nuclear capability: its inability to produce or purchase fissile material, the challenges of marrying a nuclear warhead to a missile, and the difficulty of adjusting its existing missiles to carry a nuclear payload.

Since 2002, the IAEA [International Atomic Energy Agency] has issued a series of reports detailing how Iran has covertly engaged in dozens of nuclear-related activities that violate its treaty obligations to openly cooperate with the IAEA. These activities included false statements to IAEA inspectors, carrying out certain nuclear activities and experiments without notifying the IAEA, and numerous steps to deceive and mislead the IAEA. . . .

American intelligence agencies do not know nearly enough about Iran's nuclear weapons program. However, based on what is known about Iranian behavior and Iranian deception efforts, the U.S. Intelligence Community assesses that Iran is intent on developing a nuclear weapons capability. Publicly available information also leads to the conclusion that Iran has a nuclear weapons program, especially taking into account the following facts:

- Iran has covertly pursued two parallel enrichment programs—a laser process based on Russian technology and a centrifuge process. The Russian government terminated cooperation with Iran on laser enrichment in 2001, following extensive consultations with the United States, and it appears to be no longer active.

- In February 2004, Iran admitted to obtaining uranium centrifuge technology on the black market shortly after Dr. A.Q. Khan, the father of Pakistan's nuclear weapons program, confessed to secretly providing this technology to Iran, Libya, and North Korea. Khan also sold nuclear bomb plans to Libya. It is not known whether Khan sold nuclear weapon plans to Iran.

- The IAEA reported on February 27, 2006, that Iran has produced approximately 85 tons of uranium hexafluoride (UF6). If enriched through centrifuges to weapons-grade material—a capability Iran is working hard to master—this would be enough for 12 nuclear bombs.

- To produce plutonium, Iran has built a heavy water production plant and is constructing a large, heavy water-moderated reactor whose technical characteristics are well-suited for the production of weapons-grade plutonium. In support of this effort, Iran admitted in October 2003 to secretly producing small quantities of plutonium without notifying the IAEA, a violation of its treaty obligations.

- The IAEA has discovered documentation in Iran for casting and machining enriched uranium hemispheres, which are directly relevant to production of nuclear weapons components. The IAEA is also pursuing information on nuclear-related high-explosive tests and the design of a delivery system, both of which point to a military rather than peaceful purpose of the Iranian nuclear program.

- The IAEA discovered evidence in September 2003 that Iran had covertly produced the short-lived radioactive element polonium 210 (Po-210), a substance with two known uses: a neutron source for a nuclear weapon and satellite batteries. Iran told the IAEA that the polonium 210 was produced for satellite batteries but could not produce evidence for this explanation. The IAEA found Iran's explanation about its polonium experiments difficult to believe, stating in a September 2004 report that "it remains, however, somewhat uncertain regarding the plausibility of the stated purpose of the experiments given the very limited applications of short lived Po-210 sources."

Timeline to an Iranian Nuclear Bomb

The U.S. Intelligence Community believes Iran could have a nuclear weapon sometime in the beginning to the middle of the next decade [ca. 2015]. The timetable for an Iranian program depends on a wide range of factors—such as the acquisition of key components and materials, successful testing, outside assistance (if any), and the impact of domestic and international political pressures. It also depends on the assumption that Iran will overcome technical hurdles to master the technology at some point and that its leaders will not be deterred from developing nuclear weapons in the interim.

Increasing its number of centrifuges will dramatically decrease the time required for Iran to produce sufficient fissile material for a nuclear weapon. Former Iranian President [Akbar Hashemi] Rafsanjani said on April 11, 2006, that Iran was producing enriched uranium in a small, 164-centrifuge cascade using "P-1" centrifuge technology, a basic Pakistani centrifuge design. Iran announced in April 2006 that it plans to build a 3,000-centrifuge cascade by early 2007 and ultimately plans to construct a 54,000 centrifuge cascade. . . .

Chemical and Biological Weapons Development

Although it does not have unequivocal evidence, the U.S. Intelligence Community believes Iran has an offensive chemical weapons research and development capability. The Intelligence Community reported in its November 2004 unclassified *Report to Congress on the Acquisition of Technology Relating to Weapons of Mass Destruction and Advanced Conventional Munitions*, also known as the *721 Report*, that Iran

"... continued to seek production technology, training, and expertise from foreign entities that could further Tehran's efforts to achieve an indigenous capability to produce nerve agents. Iran may have already stockpiled blister, blood, chok-

Ranges of Iran's Missiles

Russia

Turkey

Iran

Iraq

China

India

Saudi
Arabia

1,300 km
Shahab-3

500 km Scud-C

4,000 km
Shahab-4

300 km Scud-B

2000   0   2000   4000 Kilometers

TAKEN FROM: U.S. House of Representatives Permanent Select
Committee on Intelligence, *Recognizing Iran as a Strategic Threat*,
August 23, 2006.

ing, and possibly nerve agents—and the bombs and artillery
shells to deliver them—which it previously had manufac-
tured."

The Department of State drew similar conclusions in its
2005 Report on Adherence and Compliance with Arms Control,

Nonproliferation, and Disarmament Agreements and Commitments, a report that was cleared by all policy and intelligence agencies:

> "We continue to believe that Iran has not acknowledged the full extent of its chemical weapons program, that it has indigenously produced several first-generation CW [chemical warfare] agents (blood, blister, and choking agents), and that it has the capability to produce traditional nerve agents. However, the size and composition of any Iranian stockpile is not known."

> "The United States judges that Iran is in violation of its Chemical Weapons Convention obligations because Iran is acting to retain and modernize key elements of its CW infrastructure to include an offensive CW R&D [research and development] capability and dispersed mobilization facilities."

The U.S. Intelligence Community believes Iran probably has an offensive biological weapons program but lacks clear intelligence proving that this is the case. The U.S. Intelligence Community stated in its November 2004 *721 Report*:

> "Tehran probably maintains an offensive BW [biological warfare] program. Iran continued to seek dual-use biotechnical materials, equipment, and expertise. While such materials had legitimate uses, Iran's biological warfare program also could have benefited from them. It is likely that Iran has capabilities to produce small quantities of BW agents, but has a limited ability to weaponize them." . . .

One of the most disturbing aspects of the Iranian WMD [weapons of mass destruction] program is its determined effort to construct ballistic missiles that will enable Tehran to deliver conventional or, potentially, chemical, biological, or nuclear warheads against its neighbors in the region and beyond. Iran claimed last fall that its Shahab-3 missile can currently strike targets at distances up to 2,000 km (1,200 miles), including Israel, Egypt, Turkey, Saudi Arabia, Afghanistan, India, Pakistan, and southeastern Europe. It is believed that Iran's Shahab-4 will have a range of 4,000 km (2,400 miles), enabling Iran to strike Germany, Italy, and Moscow. . . .

Iran Is Destabilizing Iraq

Iranian involvement in Iraq is extensive, and poses a serious threat to U.S. national interests and U.S. troops. It is enabling Shia militant groups to attack Coalition forces and is actively interfering in Iraqi politics. General John Abizaid told the Senate Armed Service Committee on March 14, 2006:

> "Iran is pursuing a multi-track policy in Iraq, consisting of overtly supporting the formation of a stable, Shia Islamist-led central government while covertly working to diminish popular and military support for U.S. and Coalition operations there. Additionally, sophisticated bomb making material from Iran has been found in improvised explosive devices (IEDs) in Iraq."

[Director of National Intelligence John] Negroponte stated in February 2006 that Iran has demonstrated a degree of restraint in its support of violent attacks against Coalition forces in Iraq:

> "Tehran's intentions to inflict pain on the United States in Iraq has been constrained by its caution to avoid giving Washington an excuse to attack it, the clerical leadership's general satisfaction with trends in Iraq, and Iran's desire to avoid chaos on its borders."

Some Iranian assistance to Iraqi insurgents already has been provided. However, through its terrorist proxies, intelligence service, Revolutionary Guard Corps (IRGC), and other tools of power projection and influence, Iran could at any time significantly ramp up its sponsorship of violent attacks against U.S. forces in Iraq and elsewhere in the Middle East if it believed doing so would keep the United States distracted or would otherwise be in Iran's national interest. Iran's support of the June 25, 1996, truck bombing of the Khobar Towers in Saudi Arabia, a terrorist act that killed 19 U.S. Servicemen and wounded 500, demonstrated that Tehran is willing to organize attacks on U.S. personnel. . . .

Iranian Support for Hezbollah

The July 2006 Hezbollah [an Islamic paramilitary organization based in Lebanon] attacks on Israel [in which Hezbollah launched rockets at settlements in northern Israel] likely is the latest use of terrorism by Iran to advance its regional policy goals. Iran has used terrorism over the years as a means of projecting power, mostly against Israel but also against internal dissidents and other adversaries in Europe. . . .

Iran's influence over Hezbollah gives it a role in the Israeli-Palestinian peace process, making Tehran a player on an issue of global importance. Its ties to Hezbollah also provide Iran with a power projection tool—"an extension of their state," according to State Department Counterterrorism Coordinator Henry Crumpton—allowing it to authorize (or prevent) terror attacks as a way to exercise influence in the region or beyond. Iran also employs the threat of stepped-up terror attacks as a deterrent against hostile powers; the possibility that Iran might unleash its terrorist proxies against the United States and its allies undoubtedly gives pause to those who might call for aggressive action against Iran.

The extent to which Iran directed the July/August 2006 Hezbollah attacks against Israel is unknown, as are possible Iranian objectives for provoking hostilities with Israel at this point in time. Certainly, Iran could benefit if the international community's attention was diverted away from Iran's nuclear program. It is urgent that the U.S. Intelligence Community redouble its efforts to uncover any Iranian agenda behind the attacks and learn how Iran may be directing them.

> *"The 'Iranian Threat' is derived solely from the rhetoric of those who appear to seek confrontation between the United States and Iran."*

Iran Is Not a Threat to the United States and Its Allies

Scott Ritter

Scott Ritter is a former Marine Corps intelligence officer who served as a weapons inspector in Iraq from 1991 to 1998. He is the author of Target Iran *and other books. In the following viewpoint, Ritter states that Iran is not a threat to the United States, Israel, or any Western allies. He asserts that Iran has little conventional military strength and its supposed nuclear weapons program is a product of unsubstantiated speculation on the part of Western fear-mongers. In addition, Ritter claims much of the concern over Iran's supposed links to terrorism and radical Islam is a creation of American propaganda to further U.S. foreign policy and national security agendas.*

As you read, consider the following questions:

1. Ritter claims that war with what country reduced Iran's conventional military power?

2. Why does Ritter say that Iran's support of Hezbollah should not be considered a threat to U.S. security?

3. What two points, in Ritter's view, counter the myth that Iran seeks to destroy Israel?

Iran has never manifested itself as a serious threat to the national security of the United States, or by extension as a security threat to global security. At the height of Iran's "exportation of the Islamic Revolution" phase, in the mid-1980's, the Islamic Republic demonstrated a less-than-impressive ability to project its power beyond the immediate borders of Iran, and even then this projection was limited to war-torn Lebanon.

Iranian military capability reached its modern peak in the late 1970s, during the reign of Reza Shah Pahlavi. The combined effects of institutional distrust on the part of the theocrats who currently govern the Islamic Republic of Iran concerning the conventional military institutions, leading as it did to the decay of the military through inadequate funding and the creation of a competing paramilitary organization, the Iranian Revolutionary Guard Command (IRGC), and the disastrous impact of an eight-year conflict with Iraq, meant that Iran has never been able to build up conventional military power capable of significant regional power projection, let alone global power projection.

Failing to Export Fundamentalist Revolution

Where Iran has demonstrated the ability for global reach is in the spread of Shi'a Islamic fundamentalism, but even in this case the results have been mixed. Other than the expansive relations between Iran (via certain elements of the IRGC) and the Hezbollah movement in Lebanon, Iranian success stories when it comes to exporting the Islamic revolution are virtually non-existent. Indeed, the efforts on the part of the IRGC to export Islamic revolution abroad, especially into Europe and other western nations, have produced the opposite effect desired. Based upon observations made by former and current IRGC officers, it appears that those operatives chosen to spread the revolution in fact more often than not returned to Iran noting that peaceful coexistence with the west was not only possible but preferable to the exportation of Islamic fundamentalism. Many of these IRGC officers began to push for moderation of the part of the ruling theocrats in Iran, both in terms of interfacing with the west and domestic policies.

The concept of an inherent incompatibility between Iran, even when governed by a theocratic ruling class, and the United States is fundamentally flawed, especially from the perspective of Iran. The Iran of today seeks to integrate itself responsibly with the nations of the world, clumsily so in some instances, but in any case a far cry from the crude attempts to export Islamic revolution in the early 1980s. The United States claims that Iran is a real and present danger to the security of the US and the entire world, and cites Iranian efforts to acquire nuclear technology, Iran's continued support of Hezbollah in Lebanon, Iran's "status" as a state supporter of terror, and Iranian interference into the internal affairs of Iraq and Afghanistan as the prime examples of how this threat manifests itself.

Outdated Fears of Iranian Terror

On every point, the case made against Iran collapses upon closer scrutiny. The International Atomic Energy Agency (IAEA), mandated to investigate Iran's nuclear programs, has concluded that there is no evidence that Iran is pursuing a nuclear weapons program. Furthermore, the IAEA has concluded that it is capable of monitoring the Iranian nuclear program to ensure that it does not deviate from the permitted nuclear energy program Iran states to be the exclusive objective of its endeavors. Iran's support of the Hezbollah Party in

What Is Certain About Iran

Iran has an economy the size of Finland's and an annual defense budget of around $4.8 billion. It has not invaded a country since the late 18th century. The United States has a GDP [gross domestic product] that is 68 times larger and defense expenditures that are 110 times greater. Israel and every Arab country (except Syria and Iraq) are quietly or actively allied against Iran. And yet we are to believe that Tehran is about to overturn the international system and replace it with an Islamo-fascist order?

Fareed Zakaria,
"Stalin, Mao and . . . Ahmadinejad?"
Newsweek, *October 29, 2007.*

Lebanon . . . while a source of concern for the State of Israel, does not constitute a threat to American national security primarily because the support provided is primarily defensive in nature, designed to assist Hezbollah in deterring and repelling an Israeli assault of sovereign Lebanese territory. Similarly, the bulk of the data used by the United States to substantiate the claims that Iran is a state sponsor of terror is derived from the aforementioned support provided to Hezbollah. Other arguments presented are either grossly out of date (going back to the early 1980s when Iran was in fact exporting Islamic fundamentalism) or unsubstantiated by fact.

The US claims concerning Iranian interference in both Iraq and Afghanistan ignore the reality that both nations border Iran, both nations were invaded and occupied by the United States, not Iran, and that Iran has a history of conflict with both nations that dictates a keen interest concerning the internal domestic affairs of both nations. The United States continues to exaggerate the nature of Iranian involvement in Iraq, arresting "intelligence operatives" who later turned out to be economic and diplomatic officials invited to Iraq by the Iraqi government itself. Most if not all the claims made by the United States concerning Iranian military involvement in Iraq and Afghanistan have not been backed up with anything stronger than rhetoric, and more often than not are subsequently contradicted by other military and governmental officials, citing a lack of specific evidence.

No Threat to Israel

Iran as a nation represents absolutely no threat to the national security of the United States, or of its major allies in the region, including Israel. The media hype concerning alleged statements made by Iran's President [Mahmoud] Ahmadinejad has created and sustained the myth that Iran seeks the destruction of the State of Israel. Two points of fact directly contradict this myth. First and foremost, Ahmadinejad never articulated an Iranian policy objective to destroy Israel, rather noting that Israel's policies would lead to its "vanishing from the pages of time." Second, and perhaps most important, Ahmadinejad does not make foreign policy decisions on the part of the Islamic Republic of Iran. This is the sole purview of the "Supreme Leader," the Ayatollah [Ruhollah] Khomeini. In 2003 Khomeini initiated a diplomatic outreach to the United States inclusive of an offer to recognize Israel's right to exist. This initiative was rejected by the United States, but nevertheless represents the clearest indication of what the true policy objective of Iran is vis-à-vis Israel.

The fact of the matter is that the "Iranian Threat" is derived solely from the rhetoric of those who appear to seek confrontation between the United States and Iran, and largely divorced from fact-based reality. A recent request on the part of Iran to allow President Ahmadinejad to lay a wreath at "ground zero" in Manhattan was rejected by New York City officials. The resulting public outcry condemned the Iranian initiative as an affront to all Americans, citing Iran's alleged policies of supporting terrorism. This knee-jerk reaction ignores the reality that Iran was violently opposed to al-Qaeda's presence in Afghanistan throughout the 1990s leading up to 2001, and that Iran was one of the first Muslim nations to condemn the terror attacks against the United States on September 11, 2001.

Making Iran an Enemy

A careful fact-based assessment of Iran clearly demonstrates that it poses no threat to the legitimate national security interests of the United States. However, if the United States chooses to implement its own unilateral national security objectives concerning regime change in Iran, there will most likely be a reaction from Iran which produces an exceedingly detrimental impact on the national security interests of the United States, including military, political and economic. But the notion of claiming a nation like Iran to constitute a security threat simply because it retains the intent and capability to defend its sovereign territory in the face of unprovoked military aggression is absurd. In the end, however, such absurdity is trumping fact-based reality when it comes to shaping the opinion of the American public on the issue of the Iranian "threat."

> "[Air strikes against Iranian nuclear targets] have the potential to buy considerable time, thereby putting that critical asset back on our side of the ledger rather than on Iran's."

Military Strikes Against Iranian Nuclear Targets Would Slow Nuclear Progress

John R. Bolton

John R. Bolton argues in the following viewpoint that diplomatic pressure against Iran has done nothing to stall its nuclear weapons program. He insists that the United States should instead facilitate an Israeli strike against nuclear targets in Iran to help delay—even if temporarily—Iran's nuclear intentions. Bolton believes this action will thwart Iran's ambitions until a more permanent solution can be found to the problem. John R. Bolton is a senior fellow at the American Enterprise Institute, a conservative think tank.

As you read, consider the following questions:

1. How long has Iran been pursuing nuclear weapons, according to Bolton?

2. Why does Bolton believe that current economic sanctions are not deterring Iran from building nuclear weapons?

3. As Bolton states, how have the 2008 presidential candidates, John McCain and Barack Obama, responded to the Iranian problem?

Iran's test salvo of ballistic missiles [in July 2008] together with recant threatening rhetoric by commanders of the Islamic Republic's Revolutionary Guards emphasizes how close the Middle East is to a fundamental, in fact an irreversible, turning point.

Tehran's efforts to intimidate the United States and Israel from using military force against its nuclear program, combined with yet another diplomatic charm offensive with the Europeans, are two sides of the same policy coin. The regime is buying the short additional period of time it needs to produce deliverable nuclear weapons, the strategic objective it has been pursuing clandestinely for 20 years.

The Price of Delay

Between Iran and its long-sought objective, however, a shadow may fall: targeted military action, either Israeli or American. Yes, Iran cannot deliver a nuclear weapon on target today, and perhaps not for several years. Estimates vary widely, and no one knows for sure when it will have a deliverable weapon except the mullahs, and they're not telling. But that is not the key date. Rather, the crucial turning point is when Iran masters all the capabilities to weaponize without further external possibility of stopping it. Then the decision to weaponize, and its timing, is Tehran's alone. We do not know if Iran is at this point, or very near to it. All we do know is that, after five years of failed diplomacy by the EU-3 (Britain, France and Germany), Iran is simply five years closer to nuclear weapons.

And yet, true to form, State Department comments to Congress [in July 2008]—even as Iran's missiles were ascending—downplayed Iran's nuclear progress, ignoring the cost of failed diplomacy. But the confident assumption that we have years to deal with the problem is high-stakes gambling on a policy that cannot be reversed if it fails. If Iran reaches weaponization before State's jaunty prediction, the Middle East, and indeed global, balance of power changes in potentially catastrophic ways.

And consider what comes next for the U.S.: the [George W.] Bush administration's last six months pursuing its limp diplomatic efforts, plus six months of a new president getting his national security team and policies together. In other words, one more year for Tehran to proceed unhindered to "the point of no return."

Gaining More Time

We have almost certainly lost the race between giving "strong incentives" for Iran to abandon its pursuit of nuclear weapons, and its scientific and technological efforts to do just that. Swift, sweeping, effectively enforced sanctions might have made a difference five years ago. No longer. Existing sanctions have doubtless caused some pain, but Iran's real economic woes stem from nearly 30 years of mismanagement by the Islamic Revolution.

More sanctions today (even assuming, heroically, support from Russia and China) will simply be too little, too late. While regime change in Tehran would be the preferable solution, there is almost no possibility of dislodging the mullahs in time. Had we done more in the past five years to support the discontented—the young, the non-Persian minorities and the economically disaffected—things might be different. Regime change, however, cannot be turned on and off like a light switch, although the difficulty of effecting it is no excuse not to do more now.

That is why Israel is now at an urgent decision point: whether to use targeted military force to break Iran's indig-

> **American Views about U.S. Military Strikes Against Iran to Disable Its Nuclear Program**
>
> 52 percent of Americans would support U.S. military strikes
> 44 percent of Democrats would support U.S. military strikes
> 71 percent of Republicans would support U.S. military strikes
> 29 percent of Americans would not support U.S. military strikes
> 37 percent of Democrats would not support U.S. military strikes
> 15 percent of Republicans would not support U.S. military strikes
>
> TAKEN FROM: "Zogby Poll: 52% Support U.S. Military Strike Against Iran," *Zogby International*, October 29, 2007.

enous control over the nuclear fuel cycle at one or more critical points. If successful, such highly risky and deeply unattractive air strikes or sabotage will not resolve the Iranian nuclear crisis. But they have the potential to buy considerable time, thereby putting that critical asset back on our side of the ledger rather than on Iran's.

With whatever time is bought, we may be able to effect regime change in Tehran, or at least get the process underway. The alternative is Iran with nuclear weapons, the most deeply unattractive alternative of all.

America Should Not Hinder an Israeli Strike

But the urgency of the situation has not impressed [Democratic presidential candidate in 2008] Barack Obama or the EU-3. Remarkably, on July 9 [2008], Sen. Obama, as if stumbling on a new idea, said Iran "must suffer threats of economic sanctions" and that we needed "direct diplomacy . . . so we avoid provocation" and "give strong incentives . . . to change their behavior." Javier Solana, chief EU negotiator, was at the time busy fixing a meeting with the Iranians to continue five years of doing exactly what Mr. Obama was proclaiming, without results.

John McCain [Republican presidential candidate in 2008] responded to Iran's missile salvo by stressing again the need for a workable missile defense system to defend the U.S. against attacks by rogue states like Iran and North Korea. He is undoubtedly correct, highlighting yet another reason why November's election is so critical, given the unceasing complaints about missile defense from most Democrats.

Important as missile defense is, however, it is only a component of a postfailure policy on Iran's nuclear-weapons capacity. In whatever limited amount of time before then, we must face a very hard issue: What will the U.S. do if Israel decides to initiate military action? There was a time when the Bush administration might itself have seriously considered using force, but all public signs are that such a moment has passed.

Israel sees clearly what the next 12 months will bring, which is why ongoing U.S.-Israeli consultations could be dispositive. Israel told the Bush administration it would destroy North Korea's reactor in Syria in spring, 2007, and said it would not wait past summer's end to take action. And take action it did, seeing a Syrian nuclear capability, for all practical purposes Iran's agent on its northern border, as an existential threat. When the real source of the threat, not just a surrogate, nears the capacity for nuclear Holocaust, can anyone seriously doubt Israel's propensities, whatever the impact on gasoline prices?

Thus, instead of debating how much longer to continue five years of failed diplomacy, we should be intensively considering what cooperation the U.S. will extend to Israel before, during and after a strike on Iran. We will be blamed for the strike anyway, and certainly feel whatever negative consequences result, so there is compelling logic to make it as successful as possible. At a minimum, we should place no obstacles in Israel's path, and facilitate its efforts where we can.

These subjects are decidedly unpleasant. A nuclear Iran is more so.

*"An attack on Iran would be an act of
political folly."*

Military Strikes Against Iranian Nuclear Targets Would Be Counterproductive

Zbigniew Brzezinski

In the following viewpoint, Zbigniew Brzezinski contends that trying to thwart Iranian nuclear progress through military strikes would not be in the best interests of the United States. Brzezinski asserts that any attacks would lead to increased ill will against America and likely foster more acts of Islamic terrorism against U.S. targets. Brzezinski believes that direct negotiation—without the threat of military force—is the best way to resolve the nuclear issue. Zbigniew Brzezinski is a political scientist who served as a national security advisor to President Jimmy Carter.

As you read, consider the following questions:

1. What economic fallout would likely result from war with Iran, according to Brzezinski?

2. In the author's view, how is the United States already acting to unseat the current Iranian regime?

3. What "preconditions" does Brzezinski say Iran possesses that could lead it on a development path toward a pro-Western-style society similar to that of Turkey?

Iran's announcement [in early April 2006] that it has enriched a minute amount of uranium has unleashed urgent calls for a preventive U.S. airstrike from the same sources that earlier urged war on Iraq. If there is another terrorist attack in the United States, you can bet your bottom dollar that there also will be immediate charges that Iran was responsible in order to generate public hysteria in favor of military action.

But there are four compelling reasons against a preventive air attack on Iranian nuclear facilities:

First, in the absence of an imminent threat (and the Iranians are at least several years away from having a nuclear arsenal), the attack would be a unilateral act of war. If undertaken without a formal congressional declaration of war, an attack would be unconstitutional and merit the impeachment of the president. Similarly, if undertaken without the sanction of the United Nations Security Council, either alone by the United States or in complicity with Israel, it would stamp the perpetrator(s) as an international outlaw(s).

Second, likely Iranian reactions would significantly compound ongoing U.S. difficulties in Iraq and Afghanistan, perhaps precipitate new violence by Hezbollah in Lebanon and possibly elsewhere, and in all probability bog down the United States in regional violence for a decade or more. Iran is a country of about 70 million people, and a conflict with it would make the misadventure in Iraq look trivial.

Third, oil prices would climb steeply, especially if the Iranians were to cut their production or seek to disrupt the flow of oil from the nearby Saudi oil fields. The world economy would be severely affected, and the United States would be blamed for it. Note that oil prices have already shot above $70 per barrel, in part because of fears of a U.S.-Iran clash.

Finally, the United States, in the wake of the attack, would become an even more likely target of terrorism while reinforcing global suspicions that U.S. support for Israel is in itself a major cause of the rise of Islamic terrorism. The United States would become more isolated and thus more vulnerable while prospects for an eventual regional accommodation between Israel and its neighbors would be ever more remote.

Threats Impede Diplomatic Progress

In short, an attack on Iran would be an act of political folly, setting in motion a progressive upheaval in world affairs. With the U.S. increasingly the object of widespread hostility, the era of American preponderance could even come to a premature end. Although the United States is clearly dominant in the world at the moment, it has neither the power nor the domestic inclination to impose and then to sustain its will in the face of protracted and costly resistance. That certainly is the lesson taught by its experiences in Vietnam and Iraq.

Even if the United States is not planning an imminent military strike on Iran, persistent hints by official spokesmen that "the military option is on the table" impede the kind of negotiations that could make that option unnecessary. Such threats are likely to unite Iranian nationalists and Shiite fundamentalists because most Iranians are proud of their nuclear program.

Military threats also reinforce growing international suspicions that the U.S. might be deliberately encouraging greater Iranian intransigence. Sadly, one has to wonder whether, in fact, such suspicions may not be partly justified. How else to explain the current U.S. "negotiating" stance: refusing to participate in the ongoing negotiations with Iran and insisting on dealing only through proxies. (That stands in sharp contrast with the simultaneous U.S. negotiations with North Korea.)

The U.S. is already allocating funds for the destabilization of the Iranian regime and reportedly sending Special Forces

Pushing Iran Toward the Bomb

In the aftermath of a military strike, if Iran devoted maximum effort and resources to building one nuclear bomb, it could achieve this in a relatively short amount of time: some months rather than years. The argument that military strikes would buy time is flawed. It does not take into account the time already available to pursue diplomacy; it inflates the likelihood of military success and underplays the possibility of hardened Iranian determination leading to a crash nuclear programme. Post military attacks, it is possible that Iran would be able to build a nuclear weapon and would then wield one in an environment of incalculably greater hostility.

Frank Barnaby, "Would Air Strikes Work?
Understanding Iran's Nuclear Programme
and the Possible Consequences of a Military Strike,"
Oxford Research Group Briefing Paper, March 2007.

teams into Iran to stir up non-Iranian ethnic minorities in order to fragment the Iranian state (in the name of democratization!). And there are clearly people in the [George W.] Bush administration who do not wish for any negotiated solution, abetted by outside drum-beaters for military action and egged on by full-page ads hyping the Iranian threat.

There is unintended irony in a situation in which the outrageous language of Iranian President Mahmoud Ahmadinejad (whose powers are much more limited than his title implies) helps to justify threats by administration figures, which in turn help Ahmadinejad to exploit his intransigence further, gaining more fervent domestic support for himself as well as for the Iranian nuclear program.

Acting in U.S. Interests

It is therefore high time for the administration to sober up and think strategically, with a historic perspective and the U.S. national interest primarily in mind. It's time to cool the rhetoric. The United States should not be guided by emotions or a sense of a religiously inspired mission. Nor should it lose sight of the fact that deterrence has worked in U.S.-Soviet relations, in U.S.-Chinese relations and in Indo-Pakistani relations.

Moreover, the notion floated by some who favor military action that Tehran might someday just hand over the bomb to some terrorist conveniently ignores the fact that doing so would be tantamount to suicide for all of Iran because it would be a prime suspect, and nuclear forensics would make it difficult to disguise the point of origin.

It is true, however, that an eventual Iranian acquisition of nuclear weapons would heighten tensions in the region and perhaps prompt imitation by such countries as Saudi Arabia or Egypt. Israel, despite its large nuclear arsenal, would feel less secure. Preventing Iranian acquisition of nuclear weapons is, therefore, justified, but in seeking that goal, the U.S. must bear in mind longer-run prospects for Iran's political and social development.

Iran has the objective preconditions in terms of education, the place of women in social affairs, and in social aspirations (especially of the youth) to emulate in the foreseeable future the evolution of Turkey. The mullahs are Iran's past, not its future; it is not in our interest to engage in acts that help to reverse that sequence.

Serious negotiations require not only a patient engagement but also a constructive atmosphere. Artificial deadlines, propounded most often by those who do not wish the U.S. to negotiate in earnest, are counterproductive. Name-calling and saber rattling, as well as a refusal to even consider the other side's security concerns, can be useful tactics only if the goal is to derail the negotiating process.

Direct Negotiation Should Be the U.S. Goal

The United States should join Britain, France and Germany, as well as perhaps Russia and China (both veto-casting U.N. Security Council members), in direct negotiations with Iran, using the model of the concurrent multilateral talks with North Korea. As it does with North Korea, the U.S. also should simultaneously engage in bilateral talks with Iran about security and financial issues of mutual concern.

It follows that the U.S. should be a signatory party to any quid pro quo arrangements in the event of a satisfactory resolution of the Iranian nuclear program and of regional security issues. At some point, such talks could lead to a regional agreement for a nuclear weapons-free zone in the Middle East—especially after the conclusion of an Israeli-Palestinian peace agreement—endorsed also by all the Arab states of the region. At this stage, however, it would be premature to inject that complicated issue into the negotiating process with Iran.

For now, our choice is either to be stampeded into a reckless adventure profoundly damaging to long-term U.S. national interests or to become serious about giving negotiations with Iran a genuine chance. The mullahs were on the skids several years ago but were given a new burst of life by the intensifying confrontation with the United States. Our strategic goal, pursued by real negotiations and not by posturing, should be to separate Iranian nationalism from religious fundamentalism.

Treating Iran with respect and within a historical perspective would help to advance that objective. American policy should not be swayed by the current contrived atmosphere of urgency ominously reminiscent of what preceded the misguided intervention in Iraq.

"If Iran enjoyed favorable security and commercial ties with the United States and was at ease in its region, it might restrain its nuclear ambitions."

The United States Should Promote the Integration of Iran into the New Order of Arab States

Vali Nasr and Ray Takeyh

In the following viewpoint, Vali Nasr and Ray Takeyh insist that U.S. policy toward Iran is failing. The authors maintain that efforts to seclude Iran from its neighbors and increase economic sanctions will not deter Iran from pursuing its nuclear agenda or from seeking to expand its influence in the Middle East. They believe that this course of action will destabilize the region. Instead, Nasr and Takeyh claim that the United States should use economic and security incentives to convince Iran to temper its nuclear aims and help integrate it into a peaceful Middle East power structure. Vali Nasr is a professor of international politics and an adjunct senior fellow at the Council on Foreign Rela-

Vali Nasr and Ray Takeyh, "The Costs of Containing Iran," *Foreign Affairs*, January-February 2008. Copyright © 2008 by the Council on Foreign Relations, Inc. All rights reserved. Reproduced by permission of the publisher, www.foreignaffairs.org.

tions. Ray Takeyh is a senior fellow at the Council of Foreign Relations and the author of Hidden Iran: Paradox and Power in the Islamic Republic.

As you read, consider the following questions:

1. How has the United States depicted the Iranian Revolutionary Guard, according to Nasr and Takeyh?
2. As the authors explain, how have various Arab states reacted to the change of Iran's power in the Gulf region?
3. How would containing Iran possibly promote Sunni extremism in the Middle East, in the authors' view?

Over the past year [2007–2008], Washington has come to see the containment of Iran as the primary objective of its Middle East policy. It holds Tehran responsible for rising violence in Iraq and Afghanistan, Lebanon's tribulations, and [the Palestinian resistance movement] Hamas' intransigence and senses that the balance of power in the region is shifting toward Iran and its Islamist allies. Curbing Tehran's growing influence is thus necessary for regional security.

Vice President Dick Cheney announced this new direction [in] May [2007] on the deck of the U.S.S. *John C. Stennis* in the Persian Gulf. "We'll stand with our friends in opposing extremism and strategic threats," Cheney said. "We'll continue bringing relief to those who suffer, and delivering justice to the enemies of freedom. And we'll stand with others to prevent Iran from gaining nuclear weapons and dominating this region." Secretary of State Condoleezza Rice has expressed a similar sentiment: "Iran constitutes the single most important single-country strategic challenge to the United States and to the kind of Middle East that we want to see." Meanwhile, Iran's accelerating nuclear program continues to haunt Washington and much of the international community, adding to their sense of urgency.

Painting Iran as a Rogue and Intractable Nation

Taking a page out of its early Cold War playbook, Washington hopes to check and possibly reduce Tehran's growing influence much as it foiled the Soviet Union's expansionist designs: by projecting its own power while putting direct pressure on its enemy and building a broad-based alliance against it. Washington has been building up the U.S. Navy's presence in the Persian Gulf and using harsh rhetoric, raising the specter of war. At the same time, it funds a $75 million democracy-promotion program supporting regime change in Tehran. In recent months, Washington has rallied support for a series of United Nations resolutions against Iran's nuclear program and successfully pushed through tough informal financial sanctions that have all but cut Iran out of international financial markets. It has officially designated the Iranian Revolutionary Guards [IRG] as a proliferator of weapons of mass destruction and the IRG's elite al Quds Army as a supporter of terrorism, allowing the Treasury Department to target the groups' assets and the U.S. military to harass and apprehend their personnel in Iraq. Washington is also working to garner support from what it now views as moderate governments in the Middle East—mostly authoritarian Arab regimes it once blamed for the region's myriad problems.

Washington's goal is to eliminate Iran's influence in the Arab world by rolling back Tehran's gains to date and denying it the support of allies—in effect drawing a line from Lebanon to Oman to separate Iran from its Arab neighbors. The Bush administration has rallied support among Arab governments to oppose Iranian policies in Iraq, Lebanon, and the Palestinian territories. It is trying to buttress the military capability of Persian Gulf states by providing a $20 billion arms package to Saudi Arabia and the Gulf emirates. According to Undersecretary of State Nicholas Burns, one of the arms sales' primary objectives is "to enable these countries to strengthen their defenses and therefore to provide a deterrence against Iranian expansion and Iranian aggression in the future." And through a series of regional conclaves and conferences, the Bush administration hopes to rejuvenate the Israeli-Palestinian peace process partly in the hope of refocusing the energies of the region's governments on the threat posed by Iran.

An Unsound Containment Strategy

Containing Iran is not a novel idea, of course, but the benefits Washington expects from it are new. Since the inception of the Islamic Republic, successive Republican and Democratic administrations have devised various policies, doctrines, and schemes to temper the rash theocracy. For the [George W.] Bush administration, however, containing Iran is the solution to the Middle East's various problems. In its narrative, Sunni Arab states will rally to assist in the reconstruction of a viable government in Iraq for fear that state collapse in Baghdad would only consolidate Iran's influence there. The specter of Shiite primacy in the region will persuade Saudi Arabia and Egypt to actively help declaw Hezbollah. And, the theory goes, now that Israel and its longtime Arab nemeses suddenly have a common interest in deflating Tehran's power and stopping the ascendance of its protégé, Hamas, they will come to terms on an Israeli-Palestinian accord. This, in turn, will (rightly) shift the Middle East's focus away from the corrosive Palestinian issue to the more pressing Persian menace. Far from worrying that the Middle East is now in flames, Bush administration officials seem to feel that in the midst of disorder and chaos lies an unprecedented opportunity for reshaping the region so that it is finally at ease with U.S. dominance and Israeli prowess.

But there is a problem: Washington's containment strategy is unsound, it cannot be implemented effectively, and it will probably make matters worse. The ingredients needed for a successful containment effort simply do not exist. Under these circumstances, Washington's insistence that Arab states array against Iran could further destabilize an already volatile region.

The Difficulty of Shutting Out Iran

Iran does present serious problems for the United States. Its quest for a nuclear capability, its mischievous interventions in Iraq, and its strident opposition to the Israeli-Palestinian peace process constitute a formidable list of grievances. But the bigger issue is the Bush administration's fundamental belief that Iran cannot be a constructive actor in a stable Middle East and that its unsavory behavior cannot be changed through creative diplomacy. Iran is not, in fact, seeking to create disorder in order to fulfill some scriptural promise, nor is it an expansionist power with unquenchable ambitions. Not unlike Russia and China, Iran is a growing power seeking to become a pivotal state in its region.

Another one of Washington's errors is to assume that Iran can be handled like the Soviet Union and that the Cold War model applies to the Middle East. Both Israel and Arab governments have pressed Washington to contend with Iran's nuclear ambitions and since the Lebanon war of 2006 have worried about the strengthening connections between Tehran and Hezbollah. They have responded by throwing their support behind the government of Fouad Siniora in Beirut and trying to break the collusion between the Iranian and Syrian governments. Washington has been supportive, building up its military presence in the Persian Gulf and using [2007's] surge in the number of U.S. forces in Iraq to roll back Iran's gains there. But the same Arab governments that complain about Tehran's influence also oppose the Shiite government in Iraq, which is pro-Iranian and pro-American, and favor its Sunni opponents—leaving Washington having to figure out how to work with the Iraqi government while also building a regional alliance with Sunni Arab states. Washington's containment wall will therefore have to run right through Iraq and so inevitably destabilize the country as it becomes the frontline in the U.S.-Iranian confrontation.

The Reactions of Arab States

The Bush administration's strategy also fails to appreciate the diverse views of Arab states. Arab regimes are indeed worried about Iran, but they are not uniformly so. Saudi Arabia and Bahrain decry Iranian expansionism and fear Tehran's interference in their internal affairs. But Egypt and Jordan worry mostly that Iran's newfound importance is eroding their standing in the region. The stake for them is not territory or internal stability but influence over the Palestinian issue. Even within the Persian Gulf region, there is no anti-Iranian consensus. Unlike Bahrain, Kuwait, and Saudi Arabia, for example, Qatar and the United Arab Emirates do not suffer a Shiite minority problem and have enjoyed extensive economic relations with Tehran since the mid-1990s. Far from seeking confrontation with Iran, they fear the consequences of escalating tensions between it and the United States. Even U.S. allies in the Middle East will assess their capabilities and vulnerabilities, shape their alliances, and pursue their interests with the understanding that they, too, are susceptible to Iran's influence. A U.S. containment strategy that assumes broad Arab solidarity is unsound in theory.

Nor can it be implemented. For close to half a century, the Arab world saw Iraq's military as its bulwark in the Persian Gulf. Having dismantled that force in 2003, the United States is now the only power present in the Gulf that can contain Iran militarily. Shouldering that responsibility effectively would mean maintaining large numbers of troops in the region indefinitely. But given the anti-American sentiment pervading all of the Gulf today, none of the states in the region (except for Kuwait) could countenance the redeployment of a substantial number of U.S. forces in their territory. Thus, Washington would have to rely on weaker regional actors to contain a rising Iran, which is the largest country in the Persian Gulf in terms of size, population, and economy. Even major arms sales to the Gulf states could not change this reality.

Hijacking the Peace Process to Build Anti-Iranian Sentiment

Washington's reliance on reviving the Middle East peace process as the linchpin of its strategy to contain Iran is also problematic. Bush administration officials are assuming that resumed diplomacy between Israel and its neighbors will assuage the Arab street, rally Arab governments behind the United States, and lay the groundwork for a united Arab-Israeli front against Iran. But this hope disregards the fact that in their current state, Palestinian and Israeli politics will not support the types of compromises necessary for a credible breakthrough. Both Israeli Prime Minister Ehud Olmert and Palestinian President Mahmoud Abbas are too weak to press their constituencies toward the painful concessions that a viable peace compact would require. The expectations of Arab leaders far exceed those of Israel and the United States: while they have been openly demanding final-status negotiations, Secretary Rice has been talking only about creating momentum toward peace.

Even if the peace process can be successfully relaunched, the notion that Arabs see the rise of Iran as a bigger problem than the decades-old Arab-Israeli conflict is misplaced. After years of enmity, the Arab masses and Arab opinion-makers continue to perceive Israel as a more acute threat. Iranian President Mahmoud Ahmadinejad understands this well: he has been raising the heat on the Palestinian issue precisely because he wants to make headway among the Arab people and understands that they do not share the anti-Iranian sentiment of their governments. Along with his inflammatory denunciations of Israel and Tehran's assistance to Hamas and Hezbol-

The Limits of Containment

Containment of a target state is relatively easy when the United States has overwhelming military superiority and international support, as was the case after the Gulf War, despite the progressive tattering of the sanctions regime. It becomes much more difficult when those two conditions are not present and the target state moves to expand its military power and/or to mix in the affairs of its neighbors. Such is the case for Iran and North Korea at present. When target states seek to change the balance of power in their favor, the United States is faced with the choice of trying to repel the moves or to make concessions that erode containment.

Michael A. Weinstein,
"Containment or Concession:
The Eclipse of Regime Change,"
Power and Interest News Report,
June 28, 2004. www.pinr.com.

lah, Ahmadinejad's embrace of an Arab cause has garnered him ample support among the rank and file. In fact, Tehran enjoys significant soft power in the Middle East today. Washington assumes that its proposals regarding the Arab-Israeli peace process will redirect everyone's worries toward Iran; Tehran believes that current efforts will not satiate Arab demands. A careful reading of the region's mood reveals that Iran is on firmer ground than the United States.

A Self-Defeating Proposition

Indeed, it is not the Palestinian issue that will decide the balance of power in the Middle East but the fate of the failing states of Afghanistan, Iraq, and Lebanon, where Iranian influ ence has found ample room to expand. The Palestinian issue remains important to Israel's security, stability in the Levant, and the United States' image and prestige. It is also a catalyst for regional rivalries. But the Palestinian issue is not the original cause of those regional contests, nor will it decide their outcome. For all its worrying about Iran's growing power, Washington has failed to appreciate that the center of gravity in the Middle East has indeed shifted from the Levant to the Persian Gulf. It is now more likely that peace and stability in the Persian Gulf would bring peace and stability to the Levant than the other way around.

For a government that so often invokes the past to substantiate its policies, the Bush administration has a curiously inadequate grasp of recent Middle Eastern history. The last time the United States rallied the Arab world to contain Iran, in the 1980s, Americans ended up with a radicalized Sunni political culture that eventually yielded al Qaeda. The results may be as bad this time around: a containment policy will only help erect Sunni extremism as an ideological barrier to Shiite Iran, much as Saudi Arabia's rivalry with Iran in the 1980s played out in South Asia and much as radical Salafis [Sunni schools] mobilized to offset Hezbollah's soaring popularity after the Israeli-Lebanese war in 2006. During the Cold War, confronting communism meant promoting capitalism and democracy. Containing Iran today would mean promoting Sunni extremism—a self-defeating proposition for Washington.

The realities of the Middle East will eventually defeat Washington's Cold War fantasies. This is not to say that Iran does not pose serious challenges to U.S., Arab, or Israeli interests. But envisioning that a grand U.S.-Arab-Israeli alliance can contain Iran will sink Afghanistan, Iraq, and Lebanon into greater chaos; inflame Islamic radicalism; and commit the United States to a lengthy and costly presence in the Middle East.

The Need for Stability Through Integration

The Middle East is a region continuously divided against itself. In the 1960s, radical Arab regimes contested the legitimacy and power of traditional monarchical states. In the 1970s, Islamic fundamentalists rejected the prevailing secular order and sought to set the region on the path to God. In the 1980s, much of the Arab world supported the genocidal Saddam Hussein as he sought to displace Iran's theocratic regime. Today, the Middle East is fracturing once more, this time along sectarian and confessional lines, with Sunnis clamoring to curb Shiite ascendance. Again and again, in the name of preserving the balance of power, U.S. policy has taken sides in the region's conflicts, thus exacerbating tensions and widening existing cleavages. Beyond the Arab-Israeli conflict, the United States has shown limited interest in mediating conflicts, settling disputes, or bringing antagonists together. Washington sided with the conservative monarchies against Arab socialist republics, acquiesced in the brutal suppression of fundamentalist opposition by secular governments, buttressed Saudi power and the Iraqi war machine to temper Ayatollah Ruhollah Khomeini's Islamist rage. It is now courting Sunni regimes to align against Iran and its resurgent Shiite allies. Every time, as Washington has become mired in the Middle East's rivalries, its goal of stabilizing the region has slipped further away.

Instead of focusing on restoring a former balance of power, the United States would be wise to aim for regional integration and foster a new framework in which all the relevant powers would have a stake in a stable status quo. The Bush administration is correct to sense that a truculent Iran poses serious challenges to U.S. concerns, but containing Iran through military deployment and antagonistic alliances simply is not a tenable strategy. Iran is not, despite common depictions, a messianic power determined to overturn the regional order in the name of Islamic militancy; it is an unexceptionally opportunistic state seeking to assert predominance in its immediate neighborhood. Thus, the task at hand for Washington is to create a situation in which Iran will find benefit in limiting its ambitions and in abiding by international norms.

How to Put Iran at Ease

Dialogue, compromise, and commerce, as difficult as they may be, are convincing means. An acknowledgment by the U.S. government that Tehran does indeed have legitimate interests and concerns in Iraq could get the two governments finally to realize that they have similar objectives: both want to preserve the territorial integrity of Iraq and prevent the civil war there from engulfing the Middle East. Resuming diplomatic and economic relations between Iran and the United States, as well as collaborating on Iraq, could also be the precursor of an eventual arrangement subjecting Iran's nuclear program to its obligations under the Nuclear Nonproliferation Treaty. If Iran enjoyed favorable security and commercial ties with the United States and was at ease in its region, it might restrain its nuclear ambitions.

Engaging Tehran need not come at the expense of the United States' relationships with Iran's Arab neighbors. Instead of militarizing the Persian Gulf and shoring up shaky alliances on Iran's periphery, Washington should move toward a new regional security system. The system should feature all the local actors and could rest on, among other things, a treaty pledging the inviolability of the region's borders, arms control pacts proscribing certain categories of weapons, a common market with free-trade zones, and a mechanism for adjudicating disputes. For the Gulf states, this new order would have the advantage of bringing the Shiite-dominated states of Iran and Iraq into a constructive partnership, thus diminishing the risk of sectarian conflict. A new security arrangement would be an opportunity for Iran to legitimize its power and achieve its objectives through cooperation rather than confrontation. And it would allow the Iraqi government, which is often belittled by its Sunni neighbors, to exercise its own influence and so expose the canard that it is a mere subsidiary of Tehran. Saudi Arabia and Iran, the region's two leading nations, could move beyond their zero-sum competition in Iraq and press their allies there to adopt a new national compact that would recognize the interests of the Sunni and Kurdish minorities in Iraq.

A New Regional Order

None of this, however, will come about without active U.S. participation and encouragement. The Persian Gulf states will require reassurance if they are to entrust their defense to a new regional order. For Iran, whose chief competitor for regional preeminence remains the United States, there would be no reason to participate unless Washington were involved. The United States, for its part, would have to show that it is seeking not to impose a new balance of power but to uphold a regional arrangement that all the relevant regimes can endorse. Ultimately, the paradoxical but beneficial result would be a new situation in which all the Persian Gulf states would not just cooperate with one another but also endorse the United States' continued presence in the region. The strategy would serve the interests of the United States' European allies as well as those of China and Russia, all of which require stability in the Middle East and reliable access to its energy supplies.

Engaging Iran while regulating its rising power within an inclusive regional security arrangement is the best way of stabilizing Iraq, placating the United States' Arab allies, helping along the Arab-Israeli peace process, and even giving a new direction to negotiations over Iran's nuclear program. Because this approach includes all the relevant players, it is also the most sustainable and the least taxing strategy for the United States in the Middle East.

Viewpoint

> *"Advancing and achieving freedom and democratic reform in Iran would not only benefit the Iranian people but also be in America's best interests."*

The United States Should Promote Democracy and Regime Change in Iran

Steven Groves

In the following viewpoint Steven Groves asserts that negotiating a settlement with Iran over its nuclear aspirations and its support of terrorism is unlikely. Furthermore, Groves states that such a resolution would not benefit the Iranian people who are trapped in a despotic theocracy. Groves further argues that America should support attempts by the Iranians to push for democracy in their country and bring about a regime change so that a more peaceful and stable leadership can turn back the nuclear program and redress other problems. Steven Groves is a fellow at the Margaret Thatcher Center for Freedom at the Heritage Foundation, a conservative policy institute.

As you read, consider the following questions:

1. What does Groves say is "a major obstacle to the advancement of freedom and democracy" in Iran?

Steven Groves, "Advancing Freedom in Iran," *Heritage Backgrounder*, March 26, 2007, pp. 1–4, 6–10. Copyright © 2007 The Heritage Foundation. Reproduced by permission.

2. According to Groves, what is the Catch-22 that binds advocates of freedom and democracy in Iran?

3. As Groves explicates, what four agendas should the United States fund to help bring about a referendum in Iran?

Whether in Europe and the Far East during World War II or in Iraq and Afghanistan today, the United States has sacrificed greatly to advance the cause of freedom and democracy across the globe, but its greatest challenges on that front lie ahead. At the strategic center of the Middle East sits a despotic regime developing nuclear weapons that is led by a theocratic order of clerics and a president who openly courts the apocalypse. The United States currently faces few greater threats to its long-term security than Iran.

There is still an opportunity to bring about peaceful democratic change in Iran. The great majority of the Iranian people are deeply dissatisfied with the Iranian regime. If they could change the nature of their government, they would. The Iranian people's recent attempts to reform their government have been stymied by a repressive government that restricts freedom of speech, freedom of assembly, and freedom of the press.

A major obstacle to the advancement of freedom and democracy is the Iranian constitution, which institutionalizes Iran's despotic regime and restricts rather than protects the civil and political rights of the Iranian people. The United States should use its influence to pull together a coalition of dissident groups from the Iranian population under the single cause of holding a national referendum on drawing up a new constitution. Only when a representative, pluralistic government is in place in Tehran will U.S. security interests be ensured.

Repression in Iran

Promoting freedom and democracy around the world, especially in places like Iran, is in the interests of the United States. Nations governed by democratic institutions are the most responsible members of the international community. Such nations protect the basic civil, political, and human rights of their citizens, including the individual liberties that form the basis of a free society—freedom of speech, religion, assembly, and the press.

Political rights, especially the rights of the political minority, are honored in democracies. Citizens are permitted to change their government, and the government submits to the will of the people. Democracies preserve and protect the lives of their people and administer justice fairly and evenhandedly. Those accused of crimes or held prisoner by democratic governments are treated humanely and are not punished in a cruel or unusual manner. Ethnic minorities living in democratic states enjoy the same rights and privileges held by all citizens.

Few nations are more in need of democratic reform than Iran. Iran is one of the greatest enemies of freedom and human rights in the world. Dissidents and ordinary Iranian citizens who protest against Iran's hard-line clerical regime are routinely beaten, tortured, or killed or have their limbs amputated for such crimes as homosexuality, "insulting Islam," and photographing Tehran's notorious Evin prison.

Iran represses—often violently—its ethnic Arab, Kurd, and Baluchi populations. The regime also oppresses its religious minorities. For example, it routinely detains, arrests, and interrogates members of the Baha'i community—acts that the U.N. General Assembly condemned in December 2005. While Christians and Jews are officially recognized and are "free to perform their religious rites and ceremonies," they continue to be harassed, arrested, and imprisoned by the regime. The rights of non-Muslims are protected as long as the non-

Muslims "refrain from engaging in conspiracy or activity against Islam." Such protection must come as little consolation to non-Muslims who have seen their churches raided, church leaders detained, and worshippers harassed. Without outside support and assistance, the civil, religious, and political oppression of the Iranian people is unlikely to end soon.

A Free Iran Is in U.S. Interests

Advancing and achieving freedom and democratic reform in Iran would not only benefit the Iranian people but also be in America's best interests. As the September 11 [2001] attacks demonstrated, the world is becoming a smaller place. U.S. security at home increasingly depends on the advancement of free and stable governments abroad. The combination of the Iranian regime's nuclear ambitions and its continuing sponsorship of transnational terrorism, including support for Hamas and Hezbollah, creates a deadly security situation for the United States. In contrast, a free and democratic Iran would work with America to stabilize Iraq and support its transition to a pluralistic and accountable government, rather than funding Shiite militias and arming terrorists with deadly roadside bombs. A responsible Iranian government would not strive to undermine the Middle East peace process or harbor senior members of al-Qaeda.

Iran's behavior on all of these fronts will persist as long as the status quo remains intact. Promoting the advancement of freedom, democracy, and human rights in Iran should therefore be a U.S. priority, not just for the benefit of the Iranian people, but also for the short-term and long-term security interests of the American people.

The Iranian Constitution

Any discussion about advancing freedom and democracy in Iran must begin with the Constitution of the Islamic Republic of Iran. The Iranian constitution and the regime it legitimizes are the greatest obstacles to democratic change. The constitution establishes a despotic government in which all power and authority are consolidated in the hands of an unaccountable clerical regime. Additionally, the constitution restricts individual and political rights, ensuring that the Iranian people cannot challenge the clerical regime's supremacy. . . .

The advancement of freedom and democratic reform is likewise undermined by the severe restrictions placed on civil and political rights, including restrictions that are contained in the Iranian constitution. While the U.S. Constitution and Bill of Rights protect the American people from government intrusion and safeguard their fundamental rights, the Iranian constitution serves as a legal basis for the regime to oppress, in the name of Islam, the very rights that it professes to protect. Among the many rights restricted by the constitution are those that would empower the Iranian people to change their own government: freedom of the press, freedom of assembly, and freedom of association. . . .

Unrealistic Hopes of Negotiating a Nuclear Resolution

Given the despotic nature of the Iranian regime and the status of civil and political rights under the Iranian constitution, the prospect of advancing freedom, democracy, and human rights in Iran is daunting. The regime cannot be taken at its word that it will not build nuclear weapons, and no amount of inspections by the International Atomic Energy Agency will guarantee that the mullahs [Iran's religious government leaders] will not continue their efforts to become a nuclear power. Regardless of the outcome of the nuclear crisis, resolving the nuclear issue will do nothing to advance freedom in Iran.

Many experts argue that the United States and its allies should undertake a comprehensive diplomatic initiative with Iran, referred to by some as a "grand bargain." Such an initiative would proceed through an agreed framework similar to the 1972 Shanghai Communiqué, which established a structure for negotiations between the United States and China.

In addition to resolving the nuclear crisis, the framework approach aspires to address every other major dispute that currently exists between Iran and the United States, including but not limited to the Middle East peace process; Iran's support for terrorist groups; and Iran's destabilizing actions in Iraq, Lebanon, and the broader Middle East. The framework approach is laced with economic incentives and mutually beneficial assurances designed to bring a peaceful resolution to every aspect of Iran's bad behavior in the international arena. Notably absent from these grand bargain strategies are provisions for the advancement of freedom, democracy, and human rights in Iran.

While these major diplomatic initiatives are impressive in their breadth and depth, they are hopelessly unrealistic. They assume that some package of incentives will dissuade Iran from pursuing goals that define the Iranian regime—the pursuit of nuclear weapons, support for terrorism in Lebanon and the Palestinian territories, and the preservation of an Islamic government run by hardline clerics. All appearances indicate that Iran is unwaveringly determined to possess nuclear weapons for international prestige, to acquire regional dominance, to deter the regime's enemies, and to ensure the mullahcracy's survival.

The regime is unlikely to bargain away its nuclear weapons. No inducement from the United States or Europe could persuade Iran to stop supporting Hezbollah, Hamas, Islamic Jihad, and other terrorist groups. Suggesting that Iran will negotiate in good faith about the Middle East peace process is overly optimistic when its president has stated that Iran "cannot compromise over the issue of Palestine," Israel "must be wiped off the map," and "Zionists are the true manifestation of Satan."

The Problem of Censorship in Iran

Official censorship in Iran has a long and ignominious history. Shah Mohammad Reza Pahlavi and his father Reza Shah imposed strict controls on the press. Although these were lifted after the Islamic revolution, the new regime reverted to strict censorship in 1981, quashing books perceived as opposing official ideology. Publishing any book now requires a written permit from the Ministry of Culture and Islamic Guidance. Even worse, the legal framework around censorship—as unfair as it may be—is not fixed. Instead, enforcement depends on the personal views of the reviewer and on his or her interpretation of the law. Bizarrely, even if a book has been approved for publication, the prosecutor and the Special Court for the Press might still prosecute the writer or translator and publisher. Recently, the government said it would no longer allow books that discuss nihilism, secularism and feminism—it views the equality of men and women as a corrupt western idea.

Shirin Ebadi, "Democracy Demands Free Speech,"
Global Agenda, January 2006.

Change Needed for the Iranian People

The recommendations advanced in diplomatic framework approaches also will not solve Iran's constitutional dilemma and therefore will do little to nothing to advance freedom, democracy, and human rights for the Iranian people. The framework approaches explicitly reject any notion that the nature of the Iranian regime should be challenged. For example, one study states, "For a grand bargain to be possible, the United States should clarify that it is not seeking a change in the nature of the Iranian regime, but rather changes in Iranian behavior and policies." A second framework initiative states, "In dealing with Iran, the United States should relinquish the rhetoric of regime change" and instead communicate "that the United States favors political evolution: the long-range vision is an Iran that ushers in democracy itself in a meaningful and lasting manner."

The freedom of the Iranian people should not be so cavalierly discounted in the vain hope that the Iranian regime will make concessions on its nuclear program. It is in U.S. interests to advance democracy in Iran as soon as practicable, not just as part of a "long-range vision." Prior instances of similar diplomatic missteps lent political cover and economic support to the Soviet Union, helping to perpetuate its oppression of hundreds of millions. Over a billion Chinese still suffer under an authoritarian Communist regime in the name of détente. The United States should not repeat past mistakes by supporting authoritarian regimes and breeding resentment among people throughout the broader Middle East.

Bringing Democratic Change to Iran

Put simply, the current political system in Iran does not allow for peaceful democratic change. The mullahcracy's power to quash dissent and repress political rights and individual liberties is seemingly limitless. This reality places advocates of freedom, human rights, and democratic reform in a thorny Catch-22: The status quo in Iran cannot be improved without a major revision of the Iranian constitution, but the Iranian constitution cannot be amended without a change in the status quo.

The people of Iran recently attempted to change their political situation by electing reformist parliamentarians, only to have the Supreme Leader reverse their modest gains. The Iranian people are practically powerless, while the authority of the Supreme Leader and the Guardian Council is almost absolute. The formal and legal identity of the regime is the

Iranian constitution—a Gordian knot that must be cut before democratic reform can take root.

The Iranian people have no power to initiate proceedings to amend their own constitution. That power is reserved exclusively to the Supreme Leader. The constitution must therefore be revised by other means, either by transformation of the regime from within or by transformation of the regime from without. A democratic transformation of the regime could be initiated from within Iran if the Iranian people were permitted to hold a nationwide referendum on the constitution (and if the regime respected the result). Without support from outside of Iran, however, proponents of democracy inside Iran risk the fate of those who died in Tiananmen Square [China] in 1989. Only intense and irresistible pressure from the Iranian people, supported by the international community, could possibly persuade the mullahcracy to allow such a referendum. . . .

What the United States Should Do

The United States should pursue several avenues to provide the necessary tools and support to the Iranian people.

Support for a Referendum on Iran's Constitution. The regime's human rights violations and its repression of civil and political rights are merely symptoms of Iran's constitutional disease. The Iranian constitution is a cancer that must be excised. The United States should therefore direct its funding and public diplomacy efforts toward supporting a national referendum on Iran's constitution, overseen by international observers. Through the Middle East Partnership Initiative, the Administration should use funding under the Iran Freedom Support Act [of 2006] to:

- Assist the dissident community in establishing a Rainbow Civil Movement to unite the various groups interested in constitutional reform, such as women, students, intellectuals, workers, private business owners, ethnic and religious minorities, and the middle class.

- Support dissemination within Iran of articles, literature, treatises, and other information promoting a referendum on the constitution.

- Provide training for Web site creation and maintenance to the dissident community to expand its Internet outreach. This effort should include software and anti-filtering technology to counter on-line censorship.

- Covertly provide secure cellular phones and other communications devices to Iranian dissidents to aid in their organizational activities.

Legislation Supporting Regime Transformation. Any future congressional legislation relating to Iran should clearly state that the United States supports a democratic transformation of the Iranian regime. The mullahcracy headed by Supreme Leader Ayatollah [Ruhollah] Khamenei and the Guardian Council is illegitimate and should be treated accordingly. The legislation should state unambiguously that the United States seeks a peaceful change of Iran's form of government and constitution through a national referendum, not merely a change in Iran's leadership. There are no enlightened mullahs waiting in the wings to lead Iran to a bright, democratic future.

Public Diplomacy. Only when the Iranian people feel solidarity with the free world will they generate the momentum required to break free from their isolation. The United States should continue its efforts to reach the Iranian people through radio and television.

Radio Farda broadcasts news programming in Farsi into Iran, but it also airs a great deal of popular music. To be more effective, Radio Farda should instead commit a large percentage of its broadcast to serious analysis and programming relating to history, culture, religion, economics, and law, especially human rights, democracy, and the Iranian constitution. As an alternative, a second 24-hour station could be established for this purpose. Funding should also be provided for the purchase and distribution of satellite radio receivers within Iran to widen the potential audience.

Strengthened and Consolidated Financial Pressure. The U.S. Treasury Department, which has banned institutions and individuals in the United States from doing business with certain Iranian banks, should expand on these successful efforts to squeeze Iran financially. Bans on Bank Sepah and Bank Saderat have already shown positive results, in contrast to the U.N. Security Council's toothless sanctions.

The United States should also continue to press its European allies and Japan to apply economic pressure on Iran outside of the U.N. framework. European nations—especially Germany, France, and Italy—should apply massive pressure on the Iranian regime by ending government-backed export guarantees and by restricting investment.

No Security Guarantees. The United States should not give Iran any comprehensive security guarantee (a common element of the "grand bargain" approach). As part of the negotiations over Iran's nuclear program, the regime will likely demand that the United States abandon all efforts to advance democratic change in Iran. Whatever diplomatic approach is pursued in connection with Iran's nuclear program, the United States should retain the right to promote freedom and democracy peacefully within Iran.

Do Not Forsake the Iranian People

With the world focusing on the negotiations regarding Iran's nuclear program, it is tempting to relegate the pursuit of a free and democratic Iran to secondary or tertiary status, if not to abandon it altogether. While the realities of the ongoing nuclear dispute necessitate placing the goal of advancing democracy in Iran within a broader context, promoting freedom in Iran should not be completely discarded in favor of resolving the Iranian nuclear issue.

Even in the remote circumstance that Iran agrees to refrain from building nuclear weapons, the regime will remain the world's leading sponsor of international terrorism and will likely continue its efforts to destabilize Iraq. The United States needs to work diligently to resolve the nuclear crisis, but not at the expense of condemning future generations of Iranians to perpetual oppression.

> "Because Iran is one of the region's most cloistered societies, Americans rarely hear Iranian voices."

The U.S. Media Has Perpetuated Negative Stereotypes About Iran and Its People

Nina Hamedani

Nina Hamedani obtained a masters degree at the London School of Economics. She works as an intern at the Washington Report on Middle East Affairs, *in which the following viewpoint was published. Hamedani contends that American media have a distorted view of Iranians. Television and print sources, she argues, have accepted the government's view of Iranians as religious radicals bent on destroying America. However, Hamedani insists that Iranians are a highly educated and deeply cultured people who do not pose a serious threat to the United States.*

As you read, consider the following questions:

1. What incident did Iranians who spoke with Hamedani cite most often as an example of damaging U.S. involvement in the Middle East?

2. What did an Iranian woman interviewed by Hamedani want Westerners to know about the lives of Iranian women?

3. What percentage of Iranians are under thirty years old, according to the author?

Since at least the middle of the 20th century, the Middle East, including non-Arab Iran, has played a central part in the American imagination. A turning point in American perceptions of Iran was that country's 1979 Islamic Revolution (*engalab*) and the ensuing 444-day hostage crisis. Instead of being seen as an exotic foreign land, Iran was henceforth portrayed as hostile and threatening by U.S. politicians and the media. Daily Americans saw threatening images repeated ad nauseam of frantic mobs shouting, "*Marg bar Amrika!*" ("Death to America!"), turbaned mullahs, and darkly veiled women.

Since the attacks of Sept. 11, 2001, Washington has trained its sights on Iran with renewed intensity. In his State of the Union Address of Jan. 29, 2002, President George W. Bush labeled it part of an ominous "axis of evil"—a label which, bolstered by previous prejudices, unfortunately has stuck. Iran's alleged involvement in Iraq, along with its outspoken stance on Israel, theocratic government, and nuclear energy program—all vehemently opposed by the Bush administration—have become the targets of heated American rhetoric. Nor have efforts abated to translate that rhetoric into action.

Legacy of American Involvement

Because Iran is one of the region's most cloistered societies, Americans rarely hear Iranian voices. As a result, the public preconceptions go unchallenged, to the detriment of all.

Moreover, much as it might like to downplay it, the U.S. has played an important, and often negative, role in Iran's history—a role Iranians have not forgotten. In the opinion of those I spoke with during my most recent trip to Iran in the spring of 2007, the Middle East has remained an area of conflict in no small part as a result of foreign involvement. The example they cited most frequently was the 1953 overthrow, with CIA help, of the country's democratically elected prime minister, Mohammad Mossadegh, who had promised to nationalize oil and drive foreign influences out of Iran. Many Iranians were dissatisfied with Washington's hand-picked successor, Shah Reza Pahlavi, whose government was seen as being more concerned with international relations than with the well-being of the Iranian people, and were not willing to accept forced "modernization" under the Pahlavi regime.

While to most Americans, the 1979 Revolution and the rise of Ayatollah [Ruhollah] Khomeini came "out of the blue," Iranians understood it as part of an historical continuum. Had they been left to their own devices, the people of Iran could instead have carved out a uniquely Iranian identity with a representative government and religion.

An Educated, Cultured Society

Today Iranian President Mahmoud Ahmadinejad is thoroughly demonized in the U.S. media, which portrays him as uncivilized, unintelligent, warmongering, and an anti-Semitic fundamentalist. In the absence of any other "up close and personal" portrayals, these stereotypes have been extended to include Iranian men in general. Iranian women are presented as oppressed, uneducated, and downtrodden second-class citizens. In fact, they are highly educated, many having earned graduate degrees, drive alone, and are active in the professional fields of education, medicine, and business. During my visit a

The Evolution of Iranian Politics and Society

Contemporary Iran has a highly stratified society ... that will change the look of its elite leaders and its foreign policies in an evolutionary manner. Its young population will be the driving force that sets an agenda focused on economic development, cultural diversity, and political openness. The current political stage in Iran requires time to mature; it can be viewed as a transitional period in the country's long and linear historical struggle with despotism and monarchism, one that will peacefully lead to an institutionalized Iran. . . .

Islam will indefinitely remain a part, but not necessarily the ruling part, of the Iranian culture no matter how the Iranian political system might evolve. Thus, the external promotion of a secular culture in Iran is not a realistic political pursuit at this time and is likely to harm external as well as Iranian interests.

Mahmood Sariolghalam,
"Understanding Iran: Getting Past Stereotypes and Mythology,"
Washington Quarterly, *Autumn 2003.*

woman told me that she wanted Westerners to know that wearing her headscarf, or *rusari*, did not impede her life in any way.

Thanks to the availability of (albeit illegal) satellite TV, many Iranians have access to all the major U.S. media networks, which are watched primarily by the innumerable young Iranians studying English. Those I spoke with complained about the portrayal of Iran as a primitive or Third World country (*jahoneh sevom*), and characterized U.S. media reports as "propaganda" which fail to present any positive programs on Iran's religion, culture, and history. Because U.S. media are so obsessed with Islamic fundamentalism and its alleged link to terrorism, I was told, Americans are ignorant of the "real Islam" as a peaceful way to experience the comforts of wealth, health, and relaxation, even if one is sick or poor.

Iranians are imbued with a long-term view of history (*tarik*), and are proud of their cultural heritage, which includes a strong artistic tradition, from Omar Khayyam's paintings to the poems of Ferdowsi, Sa'adi, and Hafez (to name a few). It is not uncommon to hear discussions of the "golden age" of Iran—in the time of the ancient kings Qurush (Cyrus) and Darius, dating as far back as the 5th Century BC—or to the country's countless architectural marvels, such as Persepolis in Shiraz or Naghshejahan and Seeyo-sepal in Esfahan. Little of this is covered in the U.S. media.

Fears of Young Iranians

Of Iran's current population of approximately 70 million people, more than 70 percent are under the age of 30. And it's young Iranians who are most personally affected by the negative stereotypes of their country and culture. While they are serious about learning English and hope for the chance to travel abroad for higher education and work, many told me about feeling great confusion and uncertainty about their future (*ayandeh*). They not only fear that Westerners they meet will view them negatively because of the prevalent media distortions, but they are feeling internalized pressure not to validate these stereotypes with their behavior. Another source of anxiety for many young Iranian men is mandatory military service. They are understandably fearful that the U.S. will decide to attack Iran, as threatened by the U.S. administration—and by both Republican and Democratic presidential candidates—and trumpeted by the media.

Now, in 2008, it's clear that Americans' dissatisfaction with their government and foreign policy is growing. Many Americans are realizing that the administration and media have played an active hand in distorting the nature and source of the threats facing their country—a recent example being the declassification of the 2003 National Intelligence Report (NIE), with its finding that Iran is not engaged in an active nuclear weapons program.

Perhaps the dust will now begin to clear, allowing Iran to emerge from its negative spotlight.

Periodical Bibliography

The following articles have been selected to supplement the diverse views presented in this chapter.

Maziar Bahar	"Inside Iran," *New Statesman*, September 15, 2008.
Ilan Berman	"Holding the Line on Iran," *American Spectator*, October 2008.
Chip Cumin et al.	"Iranian Missile Test Escalates Tensions," *Wall Street Journal*, July 10, 2008.
Shen Dingli	"Can Sanctions Stop Proliferation," *Washington Quarterly*, Summer 2008.
Dan Ephron	"Iran Nukes: Out of Reach," *Newsweek*, September 29, 2008.
Seymour M. Hersh	"Preparing the Battlefield," *New Yorker*, July 7, 2008.
William F. Jasper	"Counting the Cost of War with Iran," *New American*, August 4, 2008.
Stephen Kinzer	"Inside Iran's Fury," *Smithsonian*, October 2008.
Thomas Powers	"Iran: The Threat," *New York Review of Books*, July 17, 2008.
Jonathan Schell and Martin J. Sherwin	"Israel, Iran and the Bomb," *Nation*, August 18, 2008.

OPPOSING
VIEWPOINTS®
SERIES

CHAPTER 4

How Are Middle Eastern Nations Addressing the War on Terrorism?

Chapter Preface

The United Arab Emirates (U.A.E.) is a small Middle Eastern nation on the southern end of the Persian Gulf. Since the terrorist group al Qaeda attacked the United States on September 11, 2001, the U.A.E. has pledged support to Washington in its grand-scale war on terrorism. Part of the emirates' motivation to assist the United States may stem from the fact that it is the most "Western" of Arab countries, or perhaps its leaders feel some sort of remorse for September 11 because two of the nineteen al Qaeda terrorists that carried out the attacks were from the U.A.E. Regardless of the reasons, the United Arab Emirates has aided U.S. military operations in the Persian Gulf region by allowing naval ships to dock in Dubai and permitting American warplanes to launch and refuel from a base near Abu Dhabi.

The United Arab Emirates' position regarding terrorism has not always been so helpful. Claiming the U.A.E.'s has at best a "mixed record on terrorism," former Homeland Security inspector general Clark Kent Ervin noted in a CNN interview that the U.A.E. "was one of only three countries in the world that recognized the [Afghanistan's] Taliban [government, which gave refuge to al Qaeda] before 9/11," and that "it was a trans-shipment point for the nuclear smuggling network that ultimately got components to Iran and North Korea and Libya." In addition, the 9/11 Commission that investigated the attacks against America reported that members of the al Qaeda network used the U.A.E.'s lenient passport certification process to gain entrance into the United States. The commission and other observers have also noted that a great deal of funding from both inside and outside the U.A.E. has passed through the emirates into terrorist hands. Michael Jacobson, a senior fellow at the Washington Institute for Near

East Policy, maintains that despite these criticisms, "the UAE has never convicted anyone for terrorism financing or money laundering."

In its defense, the U.A.E. did follow U.S. recommendations in late September 2001 to freeze the financial assets of those that Washington claimed were linked to terrorist organizations. Additionally, the government of the U.A.E. has imposed regulations on what religious leaders can preach to avoid inciting members of their schools and mosques to join extremist causes. It is perhaps for this mixed bag of successes and shortfalls that the 9/11 Commission referred to the United Arab Emirates as "both a valued counterterrorism ally of the United States and a persistent counterterrorism problem."

In the following chapter, various authors look at other Middle Eastern nations and debate their commitment to counterterrorism in a post-9/11 world. Some of the commentators see marked improvement from the heads of these Arab nations, while others note indifference and laxity. All are certain, however, that if terrorism is to be curbed in coming years, it must be reined in at the source.

| *"Wealthy Saudis remain the chief finan-*
| *ciers of worldwide terror networks."*

Saudi Arabia Breeds Terrorists

Nick Fielding and Sarah Baxter

In the following viewpoint, Nick Fielding and Sarah Baxter report that Saudi Arabia is still generating and funding Islamic terrorism. The authors contend that although the kingdom officially opposes terrorism, religious extremists and other recruiters routinely encourage Saudis to take up arms and fight in nearby Iraq. These promoters are tolerated in the kingdom, Fielding and Baxter explain, and those that are brought up on legal charges commonly escape punishment or censure. Nick Fielding is a British author and journalist who formerly worked for the Sunday Times *in England. Sarah Baxter is a columnist for England's* Sunday Times.

As you read, consider the following questions:

1. What percent of foreign fighters in Iraq are from Saudi Arabia, according to an NBC News agency?

2. As Fielding and Baxter note, how many Saudi terrorist financiers have been prosecuted by Saudi authorities?

Nick Fielding and Sarah Baxter, "Saudi Arabia Is Hub of World Terror," *Sunday Times* (UK), November 4, 2007. Copyright © 2007 Times Newspapers Ltd. Reproduced by permission.

3. As the authors report, how much money has the Saudi government given to detained terrorist suspects to help repay debts and provide family assistance?

It was an occasion for tears and celebration as the Knights of Martyrdom proclaimed on video: "Our brother Turki fell during the rays of dawn, covered in blood after he was hit by the bullets of the infidels, following in the path of his brother." The flowery language could not disguise the brutal truth that a Saudi family had lost two sons fighting for Al-Qaeda in Iraq.

The elder brother, Khaled, had been a deputy commander of a crack jihadist "special forces" unit. After his "glorious" death, Turki took his place.

"He was deeply affected by the martyrdom of his brother," the Knights said. "He became more ambitious and more passionate about defending the land of Islam and dying as a martyr, like his brother."

Turki's fervent wish was granted [in 2007], but another Saudi national who travelled to Iraq had second thoughts. He was a graduate from a respectable family of teachers and professors who was recruited in a Saudi Arabian mosque and sent to Iraq with $1,000 in travel expenses and the telephone number of a smuggler who could get him across the Syrian border.

In Iraq he was ordered to blow himself up in a tanker on a bridge in Ramadi, but he panicked before he could press the detonator. He was arrested by Iraqi police. In a second lorry, another foreign fighter followed orders and died.

King Abdullah was surprised during his two-day state visit to Britain [in 2007] by the barrage of criticism directed at the Saudi kingdom. Officials were in "considerable shock", one former British diplomat said.

A Steady Stream of Recruits

Back home the king is regarded as a modest reformer who has cracked down on homegrown terrorism and loosened a few relatively minor restrictions on his subjects' personal freedom.

With oil prices surging, Saudi Arabia is growing in prosperity and embracing some modern trappings. Bibles and crucifixes are still banned, but Internet access is spreading and there are plans for "Mile High Tower", the world's tallest skyscraper, in Jeddah. As a key ally of the West, the king had every reason to expect a warm welcome.

Yet wealthy Saudis remain the chief financiers of worldwide terror networks. "If I could somehow snap my fingers and cut off the funding from one country, it would be Saudi Arabia," said Stuart Levey, the US Treasury official in charge of tracking terror financing.

Extremist clerics provide a stream of recruits to some of the world's nastiest trouble spots.

An analysis by NBC News suggested that the Saudis make up 55% of foreign fighters in Iraq. They are also among the most uncompromising and militant.

Half the foreign fighters held by the US at Camp Cropper near Baghdad are Saudis. They are kept in yellow jumpsuits in a separate, windowless compound after they attempted to impose sharia on the other detainees and preached an extreme form of Wahhabist Islam.

Tolerating Terrorism

In recent months, Saudi religious scholars have caused consternation in Iraq and Iran by issuing fatwas [Islamic decrees] calling for the destruction of the great Shi'ite shrines in Najaf and Karbala in Iraq, some of which have already been bombed. And while prominent members of the ruling al-Saud dynasty regularly express their abhorrence of terrorism, leading figures within the kingdom who advocate extremism are tolerated.

Sheikh Saleh al-Luhaidan, the chief justice, who oversees terrorist trials, was recorded on tape in a mosque in 2004, encouraging young men to fight in Iraq. "Entering Iraq has become risky now," he cautioned. "It requires avoiding those evil satellites and those drone aircraft, which own every corner of

© 2009 Brian Fairrington and PoliticalCartoons.com.

the skies over Iraq. If someone knows that he is capable of entering Iraq in order to join the fight, and if his intention is to raise up the word of God, then he is free to do so."

The [George W.] Bush administration is split over how to deal with the Saudi threat, with the State Department warning against pressure that might lead the royal family to fall and be replaced by more dangerous extremists.

"The urban legend is that George Bush and [Vice President] Dick Cheney are close to the Saudis because of oil and their past ties with them, but they're pretty disillusioned with them," said Stephen Schwartz, of the Centre for Islamic Pluralism in Washington. "The problem is that the Saudis have been part of American policy for so long that it's not easy to work out a solution."

No One Is Held Accountable

According to Levey, not one person identified by America or the United Nations as a terrorist financier has been prosecuted by Saudi authorities. A fortnight ago, exasperated US Treasury officials named three Saudi citizens as terrorist financiers. "In order to deter other would-be donors, it is important to hold these terrorists publicly accountable," Levey said.

All three had worked in the Philippines, where they are alleged to have helped to finance the Abu Sayyaf group, an Al-Qaeda affiliate. One, Muham-mad Sughayr, was said to be the main link between Abu Sayyaf and wealthy Gulf donors.

Sughayr was arrested in the Philippines in 2005 and swiftly deported to Saudi Arabia after pressure from the Saudi embassy in Manila. There is no evidence that he was prosecuted on his return home.

This year the Saudis arrested 10 people thought to be terrorist financiers, but the excitement faded when their defence lawyers claimed that they were political dissidents and human rights groups took up their cause.

Matthew Levitt, a former intelligence analyst at the US Treasury and counter-terrorism expert at the Washington Institute for Near East Policy, believes the Saudis could do more. He said: "It is important for the Saudis to hold people publicly accountable. Key financiers have built up considerable personal wealth and are loath to put that at risk. There is some evidence that individuals who have been outed have curtailed their financial activities."

Targeting Saudi Arabia

In the past the Saudis openly supported Islamic militants. Osama Bin Laden was originally treated as a favourite son of the regime and feted as a hero for fighting the Soviets in Afghanistan. Huge charitable organizations such as the International Islamic Relief Organisation and the al-Haramain Foundation—accused in American court documents of having links to extremist groups—flourished, sometimes with patronage from senior Saudi royals.

The 1991 Gulf war was a wake-up call for the Saudis. [Osama] Bin Laden began making vitriolic attacks on the Saudi royal family for cooperating with the US and demanded the expulsion of foreign troops from Arabia. His citizenship was revoked in 1994. The 1996 attack on the Khobar Towers in Dhahran, which killed 19 US servicemen and one Saudi, was a warning that he could strike within the kingdom.

As long as foreigners were the principal targets, the Saudis turned a blind eye to terror. Even the September 11 attacks of 2001, in which 15 of the 19 hijackers were Saudis, could not shake their complacency. Despite promises to crack down on radical imams, Saudi mosques continued to preach hatred of America.

The mood began to change in 2003 and 2004, when Al-Qaeda mounted a series of terrorist attacks within the kingdom that threatened to become an insurgency. "They finally acknowledged at the highest levels that they had a problem and it was coming for them," said Rachel Bronson, the author of *Thicker than Oil: America's Uneasy Partnership with Saudi Arabia.*

Assassination attempts against security officials caused some of the royals to fear for their own safety. In May 2004 Islamic terrorists struck two oil industry installations and a foreigners' housing compound in Khobar, taking 50 hostages and killing 22 of them.

The Saudi authorities began to cooperate more with the FBI, clamp down on extremist charities, monitor mosques and keep a watchful eye on fighters returning from Iraq.

Only [in October 2007] Grand Mufti Sheikh Abdul-Aziz al-Sheikh, the kingdom's leading cleric, criticised gullible Saudis for becoming "convenient knights for whoever wants to exploit their zeal, even to the point of turning them into walking bombs".

And [in October 2007] in London, King Abdullah warned young British Muslims not to become involved with extremists.

The Money Trail

Yet the Saudis' ambivalence towards terrorism has not gone away. Money for foreign fighters and terror groups still pours out of the kingdom, but it now tends to be carried in cash by couriers rather than sent through the wires, where it can be stopped and identified more easily.

A National Commission for Relief and Charity Work Abroad, a nongovernmental organisation that was intended to regulate private aid abroad to guard against terrorist financing, has still not been created three years after it was trumpeted by the Saudi embassy in Washington.

Hundreds of Islamic militants have been arrested but many have been released after undergoing reeducation programmes led by Muslim clerics.

According to the daily Alwa-tan, the interior ministry has given 115m[illion] riyals (£14.7m) to detainees and their families to help them to repay debts, to assist families with health care and housing, to pay for weddings and to buy a car on their release. The most needy prisoners' families receive 2,000–3,000 riyals (£286 to £384) a month.

Ali Sa'd Al-Mussa, a lecturer at King Khaled University in Abha, protested: "I'm afraid that holding [extremist] views leads to earning a prize or, worse, a steady income."

Former detainees from the US military prison at Guantanamo Bay in Cuba are also benefiting. To celebrate the Muslim holiday of Eid, 55 prisoners were temporarily released last month [October 2007] and given the equivalent of £1,300 each to spend with their families.

Education the Next Generation of Terrorists

School textbooks still teach the Protocols of the Elders of Zion, a notorious anti-Semitic forgery, and preach hatred towards Christians, Jews and other religions, including Shi'ite Muslims, who are considered heretics.

Ali al-Ahmed, director of the Washington-based Institute for Gulf Affairs, said: "The Saudi education system has over 5m[illion] children using these books. If only one in 1,000 take these teachings to heart and seek to act on them violently, there will be 5,000 terrorists."

In frustration, Arlen Specter, the Republican senator for Pennsylvania, introduced the Saudi Arabia Accountability Act . . . calling for strong encouragement of the Saudi government to "end its support for institutions that fund, train, incite, encourage or in any other way aid and abet terrorism".

The act, however, is expected to die when it reaches the Senate foreign relations committee: the Bush administration is counting on Saudi Arabia to help stabilise Iraq, curtail Iran's nuclear and regional ambitions and give a push to the Israeli and Palestinian peace process at a conference . . . held [in November 2007] in Annapolis, Maryland. [The Accountability Act has yet to be taken up by Congress.]

"Do we really want to take on the Saudis at the moment?" asks Bronson. "We've got enough problems as it is."

| *"[Saudis] say they cannot defeat terror-ism by force alone."*

Saudi Arabia Is Promoting Counterterrorism

Caryle Murphy

Caryle Murphy is a news correspondent for the Christian Science Monitor. *In the following viewpoint, Murphy explains how Saudi Arabia is trying to revamp its position as a sponsor of terrorism by implementing unique rehabilitation programs for would-be jihadists. Murphy says that the Saudi government is reaching out to imprisoned terrorists and offering counseling to make them see the errors of their ways. Murphy also reports that the Saudis are offering cash incentives to those who enter and complete these rehabilitation programs.*

As you read, consider the following questions:

1. According to Murphy, who runs the rehabilitation program that services Guantanamo returnees?

2. As Abdurrahman al-Hadlaq claims, about what percent of detainees who complete the rehabilitation program backslide into militancy?

Caryle Murphy, "Saudis Use Cash and Counseling to Fight Terrorism," *Christian Science Monitor*, August 20, 2008. Copyright © 2008 Caryle Murphy. Reproduced by permission of the author.

3. What is the Riyadh Care Center, as Murphy describes it?

Khalid al-Hubayshi's career as an Islamic warrior came to an end with the siege of Tora Bora in Afghanistan. Ordered to retreat, he walked through snow for six days. He was captured by Pakistani forces, delivered to the Americans, and relocated to a cage in Cuba.

The young Saudi's break with militant jihadi ideology was not as swift. It started in Guantánamo, but ripened only after he returned home in 2005 to an unexpected reception. Mr. Hubayshi was treated to a mix of forgiveness, theological re-education, psychological counseling, prison time, and cash.

With this carrot-and-stick approach, the Saudis aimed to bring Hubayshi back into the fold of society and ensure, as much as possible, that he left behind old ways of thinking.

De-Programming Prisoners

His treatment is part of an ambitious rehabilitation program for all Guantánamo returnees and other militant inmates that is designed to counter the ideology motivating many young Muslims who have turned to violence at home and abroad.

Started in 2004, the program seeks to convince prisoners to abandon what officials call "deviant" or "misguided" beliefs. It is run by a committee that includes a religious subcommittee of about 100 clerics, a psychological-social subcommittee of about 30 psychologists and social scientists, and a security subcommittee, which determines suitability for release and monitors ex-prisoners.

It seems to have worked for Hubayshi, Guantánamo prisoner No. 155, who now lives with his new wife in Jeddah, where he works as a power plant technician. In a recent interview, he came across as affable and surprisingly free of rancor toward his former captors, and even appreciative of his own government's approach.

"We hope you learn from the past and we are going to take care of you," is how Hubayshi summed up this approach, which was extended to all 120 Saudis released so far from Guantánamo.

Changing Minds, Changing Behavior

Even though the program has its critics in Saudi Arabia, many complain that financial incentives for the former militants are unjust, the Saudis have not gone soft—they are building five new prisons. But they say they cannot defeat terrorism by force alone.

When dealing with ideology, "locking him up is not enough," says Turki M. al-Otayan, assistant professor of psychology at the Interior Ministry's King Fahd Security College and coordinator of the psychological-social subcommittee. "We have to fix his mind, and change his emotions [in order] to directly change his behavior."

Other countries, including Egypt, Singapore, Yemen, and Algeria—and the US military in Iraq—have launched similar programs, with varying degrees of success.

The Saudi program is among the most comprehensive. And while it's too soon to claim long-term success, officials say results are promising. About half of the approximately 3,200 prisoners who have gone through the program have left prison. Those who have backslid into militancy are "very few, I am sure less than 5 [percent], if it's not 1 percent," says Abdurrahman al-Hadlaq, director general of ideological security at the Ministry of Interior.

One reason for this success is that participants have been mostly sympathizers of terrorist networks who may have provided financial or logistical help; visitors to jihadi Web sites; and young men caught trying to go to Iraq or captured there.

Hard-core militants, who Dr. Hadlaq says make up about 10 percent of Saudi security detainees, have mostly declined to participate in the program. "We don't force anyone," he said, "because you are dealing with ideology."

Coping with the Flow of Jihadi

The Saudi approach contrasts sharply with US handling of accused extremists, not only at Guantánamo but also in the US criminal justice system. There, the thrust has been to impose long prison sentences, even on defendants not involved in violence.

The Saudi government's announcement in June [2008] that it had arrested more than 500 people this year for extremist activities raises the question of whether the rehab program will be overwhelmed by the jihadi undertow.

"If we don't have these efforts, you might see 5,000 [arrested] instead of 500," says Hadlaq. "Certain issues that encourage the guys to be extremists are under our ability" to control, he added. Others, like conflicts in Iraq, are not.

When a Guantánamo detainee returns to Saudi Arabia, he is interrogated by Saudi intelligence to determine what, if any, charges they face. Most have been charged with traveling to a country Saudi passport-holders are forbidden to visit, drawing sentences of one to two years, according to an Interior Ministry spokesman, Gen. Mansour al-Turki.

Like other detainees in the program, the Guantánamo prisoners meet with psychologists to discuss problems they have, what they want to do in life, and what support they or their families need.

They also have individual sessions with Islamic scholars.

"A religious adviser . . . speaks with you, and asks you what you believe and they discuss with you on what basis you believe in that, and they try to change your mind by convincing," says Hubayshi. "It's helped so many guys in the prison, they like it a lot."

The Counseling Process

When members of the Advisory Committee initially sit with a prisoner, one of the first things that they stress is that they are not employees of the Ministry of Interior or associated with the security forces. Rather, they explain that they are independent and righteous scholars. Before the government adopted this technique, it was not uncommon for families to ask clerics and scholars to visit their family members in jail and talk with them about their behavior.

In their first meeting, committee members will simply listen to the prisoner. They ask them about what they did, why they did it and the circumstances that brought them to be in prison. Throughout the process, the scholars engage prisoners in discussions about their beliefs, and then attempt to persuade them that their religious justification for their actions is wrong and based upon a corrupted understanding of Islam. The committee first demonstrates that what the prisoners were tricked into believing was false, and then they teach them the proper state-approved interpretation of Islam.

Christopher Boucek and Jamestown Foundation,
"Extremist Reeducation and Rehabilitation in Saudi Arabia,"
Terrorism Monitor, *August 16, 2007. www.jamestown.org.*

Prisoners can request which sheikh they want to talk with, or ask for a different one if they do not like the one they are first assigned, Hubayshi says.

Despite religion's dominant role in Saudi culture, Hadlaq asserted that many detainees "have limited knowledge of Islam."

This spiritual counseling is supplemented by a six-week course that covers issues such as jihad, relations with non-Muslims, the authority to issue a fatwa (religious decision), and a proper understanding of takfir, the practice of declaring other Muslims to be apostates. Passing the final exam is mandatory.

"Our main goal is to open their minds and to correct their thoughts," said cleric Abdel Aziz al-Hileyl. "We teach them to be in the middle of Islam."

Monetary Compensation

Financial incentives are a key part of the program. Hubayshi says Guantánamo returnees get monthly stipends—his is currently $800. He also was given a new Toyota Corolla and $20,000 to pay for his 2007 marriage.

The financial assistance and government help in finding jobs or furthering their education are essential for returnees to regain self-respect and avoid the temptation of their old networks, Hubayshi says.

In early 2007, the rehabilitation program launched its latest feature: halfway house to ease prisoners back into society.

Known as the Care Center, the sprawling walled property on the outskirts of Riyadh has a relaxed, camplike environment. Security is light, and the point is not to keep the prisoners in by force, but have them make responsible decisions on their own.

So far, the center has had 194 graduates, mostly would-be fighters caught heading to Iraq, or returnees from Guantánamo.

The latter group is encouraged by staff psychologists to vent their anger about how they were treated at the US detention center, but then urged to "forget about the past and try to look to the future," said Hadlaq. "You don't want them to think about . . . any kind of revenge."

"*[Lebanon's government] backed Hezbollah's 1990s attacks on Israel and refuses to interfere with the group's ongoing attacks against Israeli troops.*"

Lebanon Is a Haven for Terrorists

Council on Foreign Relations

The Council on Foreign Relations is a nonpartisan foreign policy membership organization. In the following viewpoint, the council contends that Lebanon is a haven for terrorists. The council explains that the most powerful terror organization, Hezbollah, has launched numerous attacks against Israel and U.S. troops in the region. In addition, the council asserts that the Lebanese government has done little to turn terrorist suspects over to U.S. authorities and has even appeared to sanction Hezbollah's war against Israel.

As you read, consider the following questions:

1. How many seats in the Lebanese parliament are held by Hezbollah members, according to the Council on Foreign Relations?

2. As the council claims, what treaty cemented Syria's control of Lebanon?

3. As the council relates, in what instances has Hezbollah attacked American personnel?

Is Lebanon a haven for terrorists?

Yes. Terrorist organizations operating in Lebanon include the radical Shiite militia Hezbollah, several Palestinian groups—Hamas, Palestinian Islamic Jihad, the Popular Front for the Liberation of Palestine, and the Popular Front for the Liberation of Palestine-General Command—as well as the Abu Nidal Organization, al-Jihad, Asbat al-Ansar, the Japanese Red Army, and some local radical Sunni Muslim organizations. Another militant group, Fatah al-Islam, which surfaced in 2006, has become one of the country's main security threats and was involved in a deadly clash with Lebanese troops in May 2007. Moreover, since the end of its devastating fifteen year civil war in 1990, Lebanon—a tiny mountainous Arab state bordered by Israel, Syria, and the Mediterranean Sea— had, until 2005, been largely controlled by Syria, a state sponsor of terrorism.

What is the most powerful terrorist group in Lebanon?

Hezbollah, which operates with the approval of Syria and receives massive weapons shipments and military training from its founders in Iran. It is based principally in Beirut, and effectively controls Lebanon's Shiite-dominated south, and the Bekaa Valley, allowing terrorists to move around these regions with relative impunity. U.S. officials have urged Lebanon and Syria to rein in the group. In July 2006, Hezbollah attacks on northern Israel, including the abduction of two Israeli soldiers at a border station, provoked a massive Israeli military response. Hezbollah responded by launching rockets into northern Israel. The violence came on the heels of an escalation in the Israeli-Palestinian crisis in Gaza Strip. Israel's response put pressure on the Lebanese government, highlighting both the conflicting interests of Hezbollah and Lebanon, and Lebanon's inability to disarm the group

Hezbollah is also an effective political party in Lebanon and holds twenty-three of the 128 seats in the Lebanese parliament. Since 2000, when it successfully drove Israeli troops from a forty kilometer "security zone" in southern Lebanon after twenty-two years of occupation, Hezbollah has increasingly asserted its influence among Lebanon's Shiite Muslims—the country's largest religious group—by establishing social programs, hospitals, and schools.

How did Lebanon come to be controlled by Syria?

After gaining independence from French control in 1944, Lebanon grew into a thriving trade and financial center, and its political system—based on power-sharing among religious groups—was bailed as a model of multiethnic cooperation. But in 1975, a civil war broke out between Lebanon's Muslim majority and its ruling Maronite Christian elite that left the country vulnerable to manipulation by neighboring states and terrorist groups.

Many Syrians have long considered Lebanon rightfully part of "greater Syria," and in 1976, the Arab League supported a Syrian military intervention after attempts by Western and Arab countries to mediate Lebanon's civil war failed. Tens of thousands of Syrian troops marched into Lebanon and eventually joined the Sunni-Palestinian coalition in its fight against the Maronite Christians. In 1991, Syria's control of Lebanon was cemented by the Treaty of Brotherhood, Cooperation, and Coordination, which lasted until the Syrians withdrew their troops from Lebanon in 2005.

Why were Syrian troops forced out of Lebanon?

Because of international pressure and massive protests inside Lebanon after the murder of Prime Minister Rafik Hariri in February 2005, just two months later Syria announced it was withdrawing its troops, as requested by the United Na-

Smuggling Weapons for Hezbollah

The main channel for smuggling weapons and ammunition [for Hezbollah] is Syria, where they are loaded on vehicles and sent to the Lebanon Valley through the open Syrian-Lebanese border. From the Lebanon Valley, the weapons and ammunition are transported to Hezbollah's storehouses across Lebanon, including the southern part of the country. Another channel for smuggling weapons is Turkey. That was illustrated on May 25, 2007, when the Turkish army discovered a shipment of weapons in the boxcar of a train travelling from Iran to Syria. On two occasions, the Lebanese army stopped vehicles transporting weapons from Syria for Hezbollah: on February 8, 2007, a truck with weapons and ammunition was stopped in the Beirut neighborhood of Hazmiyeh. On June 6, 2007, another truck was stopped in the Baalbek region. Those, however, were unusual incidents, rather than part of a Lebanese government policy. Another potential smuggling route is sending them by sea to the Beirut port.

Intelligence and Terrorism Information Center at the Israel Intelligence Heritage and Commemoration Center, Anti-Israeli Terrorism in 2007 and Its Trends in 2008, *May 2008.*

tions. A UN report implicated Syria in the murder, namely prominent members of President Bashar Assad's inner circle, and accused the Syrians of interfering with the investigation. Just days after the preliminary report was released in October, the United Nations passed a resolution requiring Syrian cooperation with the ongoing investigation of Hariri's death.

Have terrorists attacked Americans in Lebanon?

Yes. During the 1980s, Hezbollah repeatedly targeted Americans. In 1983 and 1984, more than 250 Americans were killed in suicide bombing attacks on a U.S. Marine barracks, the U.S. embassy, and the U.S. embassy annex in Lebanon. A U.S. Navy diver was shot during the 1985 terrorist hijacking of TWA flight 847 in Beirut, and terrorists kidnapped and held hostage several Americans in Lebanon during the 1980s.

These attacks came after the United States sent troops to Lebanon in 1982 in an attempt to quiet tension following the Israeli invasion and to help promote nation-building. Hezbollah was blamed for carrying out the attacks under the direction of its sponsor, the Islamist, anti-American Iranian regime led by the Ayatollah Khomeini. Following the 1983–84 suicide bombings, the Reagan administration withdrew U.S. troops from Lebanon.

How did Lebanon become a haven for terrorists?

Armed Palestinian groups began launching attacks against Israel from Lebanon following the Six-Day War in 1967. Hundreds of thousands of Palestinians live in refugee camps in Lebanon, and the Palestine Liberation Organization (PLO) based itself in the country after being expelled from Jordan in 1970.

The outbreak of Lebanon's civil war in 1975 caused the number of armed groups operating in the country to skyrocket. Among them was a radical Shiite militia called the Lebanese Resistance Detachments (known by its Arabic acronym, Amal), which forged an alliance with Khomeini's Shiite regime after Khomeini came to power through the 1979 Iranian revolution. In 1982, Iran created the Hezbollah militia to fight Israeli forces, which had invaded Lebanon to destroy the PLO's Lebanese base and install a pro-Israel Maronite regime in Beirut.

What has the Lebanese government done to crack down on terrorists?

Not much. The Lebanese government has cooperated in some international counterterrorism measures and has arrested al-Qaeda members. But it backed Hezbollah's 1990s attacks on Israel and refuses to interfere with the group's ongoing attacks against Israeli troops in the disputed border region known as Shebaa Farms. (Lebanon considers Shebaa Farms to be Lebanese territory under Israeli occupation, but the United Nations considers it to be a part of Syria and says that Israel has withdrawn completely from Lebanon.)

Lebanon has also refused U.S. demands to turn over Lebanese terrorists involved in the 1985 hijacking of TWA flight 847 and in the abduction, torture, and murder of U.S. hostages from 1984 to 1991. At the same time, the regime has only limited influence over Hezbollah and Palestinian militants. Moreover, it lacks control of some of Beirut and of the lawless, drug-ridden Bekaa Valley, as well as of many Palestinian refugee camps and the southern border region.

"Lebanon is performing well on a front it ironically has little experience in: counterterrorism."

Lebanon Is Promoting Counterterrorism

Bilal Y. Saab

Bilal Y. Saab states in the following viewpoint that the Lebanese people are working to reduce radicalism within their country. According to Saab, public officials are reaching out to clerics and local leaders to make sure their constituents do not embrace extremist views. The parliament is also organizing funding for education and health projects to give people more opportunities and to keep them from turning to radicalism out of desperation. Bilal Y. Saab is a senior research assistant at the Saban Center for Middle East Policy at the Brookings Institution, a public policy institute in Washington, DC.

As you read, consider the following questions:

1. What is the value of the development projects meant to improve health and education in Tripoli and northern Lebanon, according to Saab?

2. As Saab explains, what is Dar al Ifta'?

3. As the author reports, what is UNRWA doing to aid the victims of the Nahr al Bared conflict?

In spite of its ongoing political crisis, an institutionally crippled Lebanon is performing well on a front it ironically has little experience in: counterterrorism.

[In March 2008] five months after the Lebanese army's bloody though ultimately successful baffle in the North against the al Qaeda-inspired group, Fatah al Islam, Lebanese are still concerned about a repeat of the scenario of Nahr al Bared in another Palestinian refugee camp[1]. And they have every right to worry.

The militant Salafi [a Sunni Muslim sect] current in Lebanon may have suffered a heavy blow in Nahr al Bared, but given its fluidity and the favourable circumstances it operates in—an acutely polarised political environment with heightened sectarian tensions—it is capable of regrouping and finding new leaders. Al Qaeda in Iraq still has its eyes on Lebanon and the Syrian-Lebanese borders are yet to be secured.

Curbing Militancy

But there is stronger reason for optimism. The recent efforts and initiatives by Lebanese public officials, civil society groups, and official religious institutions aimed at curbing the radicalisation current in the North suggest that the country as a whole is starting to think strategically about the threat of Salafi militancy.

The healthy consensus inside the Lebanese military and security institutions on the limitations of the use of force as a means to neutralize the threat of militant radicalism suggests that the counterterrorism campaign is moving in the right di-

---

1. In May 2007 Lebanese soldiers shelled the Palestinian camp at Nahr al Bared in retaliation for an attack against an army checkpoint by Fatah al Islam militants based in the camp.

rection. Most Lebanese public officials are becoming aware of the tenet that Lebanon's most potent antidote to extremist and militant ideology involves a socio-economic vision that is rooted in policies of balanced development.

[In early 2008], Parliamentary majority leader Saad Hariri announced the launch of $52 million worth of major developmental, educational and health projects in Tripoli, Akkar and other regions in the North (initially, those projects were slated to be carried out by the Lebanese state, but funding was severely lacking due to the budget deficit).

Meanwhile, the newly-elected Lebanese Mufti of Tripoli and the North, Sheikh Malek Al Sha'ar (the highest ranking Sunni religious scholar), declared the promulgation of a new comprehensive program for Dar al Ifta', the Sunni religious establishment in Lebanon, which aims at creating a directorate for religious education tasked with supervising Islamic schools, colleges and institutes, and an advisory board consisting of all Islamic parties and groups in the North. This directorate should be of great help in making sure Islamic groups' activity in the North does not stray or flirt with extremism.

Seeking Help Inside and Outside Lebanon

At the Lebanese internal security forces (ISF) directorate, Major General Ashraf Rifi met with a large delegation of Sunni preachers and religious scholars as well as directors and presidents of Salafist organisations and institutes in the North. The purpose was to start a dialogue and form a cooperative relationship with these individuals and bodies, whose access to Sunni Muslim constituencies and role in convincing extremist elements to snub extremism and militancy is critical.

The international community's efforts in helping Lebanon recover from the Nahr al Bared fiasco should not be discounted either. The most important actor is UNRWA [United Nations Relief and Works Agency], which has been working with some 20 non-governmental organisations to implement

Location of Nahr al Bared

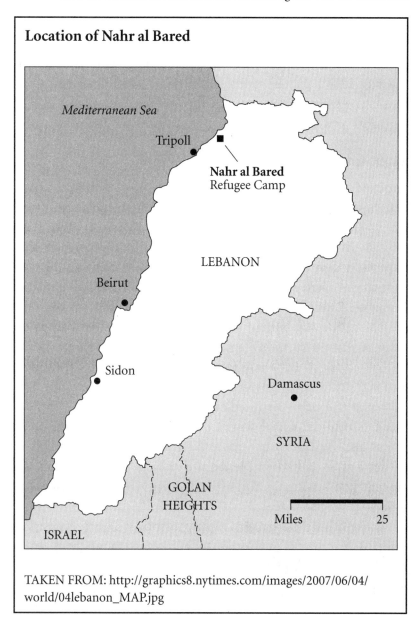

Mediterranean Sea

Tripoll ●

Nahr al Bared
Refugee Camp

LEBANON

Beirut ●

Sidon ●

Damascus ●

SYRIA

GOLAN HEIGHTS

Miles 25

ISRAEL

TAKEN FROM: http://graphics8.nytimes.com/images/2007/06/04/world/04lebanon_MAP.jpg

preventive measures for the children of Nahr al Bared, such as psychological and recreational activities. UNRWA has also trained about 200 teachers to identify the signs of trauma and refer students for help.

217

A donor conference is expected to be held in the second half of April [2008] to raise money for the reconstruction of Nahr al Bared. Foreign governments such as Saudi Arabia and Norway, and Lebanese political parties, including Hariri's Future Movement, have also provided substantial financial and logistical assistance to Nahr al Bared's reconstruction process.

The State Must Act as One

Shocked by the eye-opening experience of Nahr al Bared, Lebanese society seems determined to erase the memory of [the 2007] summer and make sure that scenario never happens again. While some praiseworthy preventive measures have been devised since then by an amalgam of local and foreign actors, they remain largely outside the boundaries of the Lebanese state.

To tap its full potential, the counter-terrorism campaign must be owned by the Lebanese state. Such a campaign should be viewed by all Lebanese (and the international community) as a collective, as opposed to a particularistic effort. Only the state and the large resources it can offer in terms of employment, education, social security, and general welfare can neutralise and ultimately eliminate the threat of militant religious extremism in Lebanon. Hence the critical need to break the current political stalemate and immediately reactivate all Lebanese state institutions.

If the Iraqi experience is of any lesson, al Qaeda thrives on political vacuums and looks to exploit societal fault lines. Lebanon should know better.

> *"Yemen itself is on a dagger's edge, precariously balanced between forces of modernization and the pull of powerful traditionalists."*

Yemen's Counterterrorism Efforts Have Had Mixed Results

Kevin Whitelaw

In the following viewpoint, Kevin Whitelaw argues that Yemen has stepped up its counterterrorism tactics but that its successes have been hobbled by government corruption and negligence. According to Whitelaw, the Yemeni government has a history of relations with militant bands, and it has struggled in recent years to impose its own independent will to crack down on extremism. The government also does not have the full faith of its people because of a poor economy and lagging reforms. Without popular support, Whitelaw fears that the Yemeni government will not effectively be able to stem the tide of radicals that either come out of Yemen or pass through its borders. Kevin Whitelaw is a senior writer for U.S. News & World Report.

As you read, consider the following questions:

1. What happened during the February 2006 prison break in Yemen, as Whitelaw describes it?
2. As Whitelaw reports, how many guns are estimated to be in private hands in Yemen?
3. Why is Yemen not getting much foreign aid in recent years, according to the author?

The roar from the shoulder-fired rocket echoes off the jagged peaks, followed by the steady crackling of automatic weapons. Systematically, the Yemeni snipers, prone against the dusty desert terrain, lay down cover fire for an assault on a cluster of tents believed to be a terrorist camp. Tufts of colored smoke mark the position of a ground assault team as the disciplined marksmen fire deeper into the camp.

This time, the assault is an exercise, but Yemen's elite Counterterrorism Unit [CTU] has successfully carried out several high-risk operations against suspected terrorists and kidnappers. Portraits of six fallen soldiers, the unit's "martyrs," hang on the walls of their barracks. "They are without a doubt the bravest guys I have ever worked with," says Ed, a U.S. Army trainer on his second tour in Yemen. *U.S. News* was granted rare access to the CTU, a four-year-old quick-reaction unit in the Interior Ministry that has gained skills ranging from close-quarters combat and descending from helicopters on ropes to mountaineering. "With American training, they have gone from basic levels to become professionals," says Lt. Col. Abdul Rahman al-Mahweeti, the commander of the 140-man force.

Balanced Between Old and New

This elite unit is at the vanguard of Yemen's efforts to take on terrorism. As the ancestral homeland of Osama bin Laden, this desperately poor and deeply Islamic nation nestled at the tip of the Arabian peninsula has become one of America's most unexpected allies in counterterrorism. A land of gun-toting tribal factions, age-old smuggling routes, and desert villages perched in centuries-old defensive positions on high buttes, Yemen feels like a place frozen in time. The earthen houses in this ancient walled city date back to before the 11th century, and most Yemeni men still wear a *jambiya*, the traditional curved dagger, strapped to their waists.

Today, Yemen itself is on a dagger's edge, precariously balanced between forces of modernization and the pull of powerful traditionalists. In the West, Yemen may be best known for its recent history of tribal kidnappings of tourists, the 2000 al Qaeda attack on the USS *Cole*, and the ubiquitous chewing of khat, a mildly narcotic leaf. But the government has helped roll up several al Qaeda cells and, at least until a recent prison break, generally allayed western fears that terrorists would find sanctuary in the large tracts of lawless, tribal lands.

A Nation Near Collapse

These days, though, Yemen is facing its own crisis, the result of deepening poverty and a government in denial about the depth of reforms needed to survive. In the past year [2007–2008], the United States and the World Bank have slashed their modest aid programs to Yemen, increasingly fed up with a bureaucracy that is one of the most corrupt in the world. "Yemen is teetering on the edge of failed statehood," warns one U.S. official. "It will either become a Somalia or get serious about transforming." For a nation awash in guns and crisscrossed by well-worn smuggling routes, the threat is grave.

So far, the worst has not materialized, perhaps because Yemen has been motivated by its own suffering. The country was probably al Qaeda's first victim, when militants bombed two hotels in Aden being used by U.S. soldiers on their way to Somalia in 1992. The bombing of the USS *Cole*, which killed 17 U.S. sailors, sent Yemen's fragile economy even deeper into free fall. "The terrorists dealt blows to us before anyone else," says Rashid Muhammad al-Alami, the minister of interior. "When we fight terrorism, we fight it in pure self-defense." President Ali Abdullah Saleh echoed a similar sentiment in an interview. "There is no backing away from the fight against terrorism," he said. "There is no halt."

Such commitment makes [February 2006's] brazen prison break particularly embarrassing. Twenty-three prisoners, including 13 convicted al Qaeda fighters, tunneled out of their cells; U.S. officials say they clearly had inside help. One of them—convicted *Cole* bomber Jamal Badawi—had escaped once before and was recaptured 11 months later. "The longer they remain at large, the more the threat level rises," says a senior U.S. official. The incident raised new doubts about Yemen's reliability. "At best," the official says, "it was a combination of negligence, stupidity, and greed."

Counterterrorism Improvements

Despite such lapses, cooperation on counterterrorism has largely improved. A major turning point came when Yemeni security forces turned up plotters who wanted to target Saleh's personal airplane. The pre-9/11 [2001] al Qaeda leadership in Yemen has been purged; in the most spectacular incident, the group's former leader in Yemen, Qaed al-Harethi, was killed deep in the desert by a missile fired from an unmanned U.S. Predator drone in 2002, apparently with Yemen's acquiescence.

Yemen has also created a Coast Guard that, with U.S. support, is beginning to patrol the nation's ports and its long, jagged coastline. "Now, as ships start to feel safer, they are starting to return," says Col. Lotf al-Baraty, the Coast Guard director in Aden. Still in its infancy, the Coast Guard will soon try to police some of the world's wildest smuggling waterways, across the Gulf of Aden from lawless Somalia. "As they stop more smugglers and illegal immigrants," says Cmdr. Scott Cull, the U.S. naval attaché in Yemen, "it makes it more difficult for the terrorists to get through."

All these efforts have paid off. *U.S. News* has learned that Yemen has helped foil three al Qaeda-related plots since late 2004, including one planning attacks in neighboring Saudi Arabia. Another cell of nearly a dozen included several fighters who had returned from Iraq, apparently under the direction of Abu Musab Zarqawi [the head of al Qaeda in Iraq]. Officials believe that Zarqawi was trying to build a long-term presence in Yemen but that his operatives became restless and began plotting more immediate attacks on targets including the Sheraton Hotel in Aden and the U.S. Embassy in Sana. The group was captured after U.S. intelligence passed a tip to Yemeni security forces. "This was a serious group," says a U.S. diplomat. "You just wonder how many others are out there."

For Yemen, the conflict in Iraq dredges up an alarming parallel. Yemenis vividly remember the aftermath of the long battle against the Soviet occupation of Afghanistan and how the battle-hardened Yemeni volunteers who returned carried out some of al Qaeda's earlier attacks. Now, several hundred Yemenis are estimated to have traveled to Iraq to fight in the past three years. "We are waiting for when the war is finished in Iraq. We have to be ready," says Col. Yahya Saleh, the chief of staff for the Central Security Force (which includes the Counterterrorism Unit) and a nephew of the president. "If they come back, they will come back with more hate, and they will have been trained there, in explosives and other skills." The government has started to crack down, stopping young men at the airport on their way to countries like Syria.

A Need to Focus on the Economy and Democracy

But this effort is hobbled by Yemen's history of cozy relationships with some of these militants and its paltry infrastructure. The government doesn't have a master database listing Yemeni citizens; even passport records are spotty. The government has pledged to curtail the thriving black market for small arms and explosives, but results have been limited. U.S.

Obstructing the USS *Cole* Investigation

While Sana'a [the capital of Yemen] cooperated in the investigation of the *Cole* incident [in October 2000 terrorists rammed a small boat loaded with explosives into the USS destroyer *Cole*, killing 17 U.S. sailors] U.S. authorities were not entirely satisfied with the Yemeni response. Saleh initially denied that "terrorists" had conducted the attack; later, Yemen suggested that the U.S. bore partial responsibility for it, having trained terrorists in Afghanistan in the 1980s. ABC News reported that a Yemeni security surveillance camera that might have filmed critical evidence had been pointed in the wrong direction, and that a tape turned over to the FBI authorities by Yemeni officials might have been partly erased. FBI officials complained of lack of cooperation from the Yemenis, who insisted on controlling the investigation, and for security reasons the bureau conducted its own inquiry from U.S. ships offshore. A London-based "expert on the region" who had lived for six years in Yemen told ABC: "The FBI and Scotland Yard are clever enough to know that the Yemen government has been feeding these people" responsible for the attack.

Gary Leupp, "The 'War on Terrorism' in Yemen," Counterpunch, *May 20, 2002. www.counterpunch.org.*

officials confronted President Saleh with evidence that guns sold to Yemen's Ministry of Defense ended up in the arms of terrorists who stormed the U.S. Consulate in Jidda, Saudi Arabia, in late 2004 and killed five people. "The worrisome thing is that there is a network, and Yemen could possibly be a one-stop shop because of the availability of weapons and people who could be recruited," says one U.S. diplomat.

Indeed, Yemen's alarming poverty—and the rising despair among its people—threaten to overshadow the tactical partnership. "By focusing on security, the United States is swimming in a sea of results while missing an ocean of failures," says Nabit Sabaie, a leading independent Yemeni journalist. Nearly half of Yemenis subsist on less than $2 a day, and unemployment continues to grow. Despite its oil resources, Yemen ranks 151 out of 177 nations on the United Nations human development index, which measures economic, educational, and health indicators. And with the population growing so fast that the size of this nation of 20 million will double in 17 years, Yemenis fear that any improvements are a long way off. "I'm afraid our people are not going to have the patience," says Mohammed Abdul Malek al-Mutawakil, a political science professor and opposition politician. . . .

U.S. officials admit that for several years following September 11 [2001], their diplomacy with Yemen focused almost exclusively on terrorism. Now, amid increasing alarm about the nation's future, U.S. diplomats are adjusting their efforts in Yemen to focus more on issues like democracy, freedom of speech, economic reform, and, especially, anticorruption. "This is a country that is really in the balance," says Thomas Krajeski, the U.S. ambassador to Yemen. "There is a risk here for failure, and there is a chance of success. It is our job to give them all the help we can, but they have to make some hard decisions now." Privately, U.S. diplomats are blunter: "We're not going to give them a pass anymore." . . .

Backsliding on Government Reform

Yemen has always been one of the most traditional Islamic countries, in part because of its isolation. But in recent years, more radical forms of Islam have begun to seep in. One factor was the return of the hardened mujahideen from Afghanistan, some of them with ties to al Qaeda. Another was the arrival of a veritable army of Yemeni laborers expelled from Saudi Arabia in the wake of the Gulf War (after Yemen backed Saddam Hussein). Many of these returning expatriates brought the Saudis' ultraconservative brand of Islam back with them.

It is also hard [for the government] to control an unruly country with complicated tribal relationships and an estimated 60 million guns in private hands (or three for every man, woman, and child). That doesn't even include the weapons trade, which U.S. officials believe includes planeloads and shiploads of weapons moving through the nation. (It is difficult to overstate the gun culture in Yemen. Take Nasser, a taxi driver in Sana, who proudly lists the weapons he keeps in his house: AK-47s, pistols, grenades, even tear gas—to control his wife and kids if they protest, he jokes. He recalls the time that he loaned an empty family house to a friend of his. When the owner, his uncle, returned, he asked, "Did you take the land mine out of the living room?")

Amid all this, Yemen has somehow managed to remain one of the most democratic nations in the (admittedly autocratic) Middle East—and one of the very few with a relatively free press. The government tolerates a raft of opposition parties and independent newspapers. Yemenis, for the most part, feel free to criticize the government, and even Saleh, in public. . . .

Still, it's not clear how much the government is capable of changing. The democratic reforms all stop short of threatening Saleh's rule; in the last election, he won 96 percent of the vote. The state maintains its monopoly on radio and television stations—perhaps the most influential media in this predominantly illiterate society. The government has also been backsliding on press freedom in recent months, as more journalists are being harassed and several newspapers have been shuttered in recent weeks.

Yemen is not getting all that much help through foreign aid these days, either. Donors are growing increasingly frustrated with the lack of progress and the overriding problem of corruption, leading to large cuts in aid this past year. "We are giving them just enough to maintain the status quo," says one U.S. official. "They need aid that's transformational—billions of dollars that they're not going to get. We won't increase it because the leadership is just not there." . . .

Roots of Fanaticism

At the same time, there is a fear that U.S. leverage in Yemen might be diminishing. High oil prices have lessened the influence of foreign aid money on the government's decision making. "Where are the incentives for the president and the government to modernize and push for more democracy?" asks [Yemeni senator Mohamed al-] Tayeb, who is critical of the recent cuts in aid. There has also been some domestic backlash to the government's cooperation with Washington on counterterrorism, given the anger over Yemeni detainees in Guantanamo Bay and U.S. policy in Iraq and Israel. "It all creates public opinion that is not in favor of, or is even hostile to, any cooperation between the American and Yemeni governments," says Alami, the interior minister.

The security situation has also made it more difficult for U.S. diplomats to reach out to Yemenis. Face-to-face meetings are difficult, with U.S. officials ensconced inside their fortress-like embassy compound. "They don't trust us when we say we're here to help them," says one U.S diplomat. "There are liberal, modern, western-oriented people, and they still don't trust us."

All of this is part of a deeper battle. "The real conflict in the country is not between the government and the opposition but is between traditional powers still locked in the 19th century and the forces of modernization that try to grope their way into the modern age," says Mohammed al-Sabri, a leading figure in the opposition. "The traditional forces are besieged, but when your room for maneuver has shrunk, you become very tense and aggressive." He points to a simmering rebellion, fueled by radical Islamists, in the northern town of Sadah, where hundreds of soldiers and rebels were killed last year [2007]. "I expect more dangerous risks in Yemen—extremism and fanaticism," he says. "But it's not related to religion. It comes out of the failure to satisfy life's needs."

Sabri places his hopes in reform. And Yemen's government is starting to talk a good game. "The state and the government are moving ahead with reforms—political reforms, judicial reforms, economic reforms, anticorruption reforms, counterterrorism," says President Saleh. "The country is moving toward modernization." For many, the upcoming local and presidential elections will be a test. And the stakes are high. "What we are afraid of is that the Yemeni people will lose hope in elections as a means of change," Sabri says, "because this is what the traditional forces want."

Periodical Bibliography

The following articles have been selected to supplement the diverse views presented in this chapter.

Abdullah F. Ansary — "Combating Extremism: A Brief Overview of Saudi Arabia's Approach," *Middle East Policy*, Summer 2008.

Jonathan Broder — "UAE's Allegiances Still Cause Tension," *CQ Weekly*, February 27, 2006.

The Economist — "Jihadist Blowback?" October 4, 2008.

Kay Bailey Hutchison — "Pakistan's Progress," *Wall Street Journal*, March 11, 2008.

Jay Nordlinger — "Syrian Hopes," *National Review*, May 5, 2008.

Bruce Riedel and Bilal Y. Saab — "Al Qaeda's Third Front: Saudi Arabia," *Washington Quarterly*, Spring 2008.

Anthony Skinner — "A State on Alert," *Middle East*, October 2005.

Robert Spencer — "Which Side Are the Saudis On?" *Human Events*, March 10, 2008.

Peter Willems — "The Right to Bear Arms," *Middle East*, March 2005.

For Further Discussion

Chapter 1

1. Since the terrorist attacks of September 11, 2001, the United States, under the George W. Bush administration, has embarked on a policy of promoting democratic reform as one facet of the larger war against terrorism. After reading the viewpoint by George W. Bush, arguing that democratic reform will benefit the Middle East, and in turn, the United States, explain whether you believe this argument. What historical example does Bush refer to support his argument? Do you think that this comparison is accurate? On the other hand, Peter Berkowitz argues that promoting democracy will actually turn people against the concept, and he insists that promoting liberty is something different and preferable to the promotion of democracy. Do you agree with his argument? Construct your own argument as to whether or not the United States should be promoting democracy in the Middle East, and support your views using evidence from the viewpoints.

2. The Iraq War has been a contentious issue in American society since the United States and its allies invaded the country in March 2003. Now, over five years later, the debate has shifted from whether it was right to invade to how long U.S. troops should be occupying the country. Bruce Bartlett argues that the United States' occupation of the country is only draining American resources and further destabilizing Iraq. Victor Davis Hanson argues, on the other hand, that evacuating Iraq now would leave the country worse than when the coalition first invaded. Whose argument do you find more convincing? Does

Bartlett's admission that he first supported the war change how you see his negative view of the conflict now?

3. Israel is often referred to as America's closest ally in the Middle East. However, the Palestinian-Israeli conflict and the larger Arab-Israeli conflict has led to increasing debate over whether this relationship is beneficial or harmful to the United States. After reading the last two viewpoints of Chapter 1, conduct some further research into the origins of the Palestinian-Israeli conflict. Do you feel that the United States' relationship with Israel negatively impacts U.S. relations with the larger Arab world? Should the United States distance itself from Israel, or is Israel an important ally in a region full of instability? Explain your answer using quotes from the viewpoints and the articles that you find on your own.

Chapter 2

1. In his viewpoint, Marwan Muasher states that if peace is to be achieved between Palestinians and Israelis, the moderate Arab world must be active in helping to broker a peace plan and not allow extremist viewpoints to dominate the conversation. Ghada Karmi says that no peace plan is possible because Israel actively impedes any efforts to engage both sides. Does it seem to you, based on these arguments, that the extremist Muslims or Israel is a larger roadblock to peace? Consider these questions in framing your answer: Is either side ever justified in its actions? Is it acceptable for Israel to forcefully occupy land where Palestinians live and build settlements and a wall for protection? Is it ever okay for Palestinian terrorists to use violence against what they see as a war against their people? Use quotes from the viewpoints, and additional sources if needed, to support your claims.

2. After elections in 2006, the Palestinian parliament has been dominated by a majority of representatives from the

Hamas party, unseating the previously ruling Fatah party. Consider the viewpoints by Henry Siegman, arguing for the capability of Hamas to achieve a peace plan, and Dennis Ross, arguing that Fatah must defeat Hamas in the future if peace is to be achieved. Which of these two viewpoints do you find more valid? Can Hamas broker a peace between Israel and Palestine, or are its violent, fundamentalist factions too strong to overcome? Now, reread the first two viewpoints of Chapter 1, arguing for and against the promotion of democracy in the Middle East. If Hamas, a group that has been labeled a terrorist organization, can win democratic elections, should democracy be promoted? Is Hamas only a terrorist organization, or does it provide individuals in Palestine with valuable services that other parties have been unable to offer? Is it more important to have democratic elections, regardless of the outcome, or is it preferable to have leadership in place that is sympathetic to Israeli and American causes?

3. Newt Gingrich maintains in his viewpoint that defeating terrorism is the best method of achieving peace between Israelis and Palestinians. He argues that Palestinians must step up and gain control over those who promote violence against civilians. Consider this argument along with the others in the chapter, and reread Michael Tarazi's argument that the Israelis and Palestinians should share one democratic state. Do you believe that this is possible? Can the two sides come together and govern as one nation? Is defeat of terrorism a necessary first step in a one-state solution? Use evidence from the viewpoints throughout the chapter to support your conclusion.

Chapter 3

1. The U.S. House of Representatives Permanent Select Committee on Intelligence insists that Iran is a threat to U.S. security and the security of the Middle East chiefly be-

cause of its assumed intention of developing an extensive weapons of mass destruction program. After reading the committee's viewpoint and the opposing viewpoint by Scott Ritter, explain how likely you think it is that Iran would build and deploy a nuclear weapon. Be sure to consider what consequences would result from Iran's launch of a nuclear weapon or the sale of a nuclear device to terrorists bent on using such a weapon against the United States or its allies.

2. Zbigniew Brzezinski lists four compelling reasons why the United States should avoid launching preemptive strikes against Iranian nuclear targets. After reading this viewpoint and John R. Bolton's viewpoint, do you think these compelling reasons should deter proposed strikes if Iran gets close to building a nuclear weapon? Explain why or why not.

3. Steven Groves argues that supporting a regime change in Iran is the only way that the United States can prevent Iran from continuing its nuclear weapons program and, more importantly, help the people of Iran escape oppression. Do you believe Groves' recommended strategy for achieving regime change would work? Explain why or why not. If you do not think regime change is the answer, do you agree with Vali Nasr and Ray Takeyh that helping Iran integrate and feel more secure in the region will bring about the end of the Iranian weapons program?

Chapter 4

1. Caryle Murphy claims that Saudi Arabia is working to curb terrorism. Do you believe these attempts at counterterrorism will be enough to thwart the types of terrorist activities that Nick Fielding and Sarah Baxter attribute to Saudi Arabia? Explain your answer.

2. Caryle Murphy reports on how Saudi Arabia is using rehabilitation to deprogram terrorists and would-be terror-

ists. Bilal Y. Saab states that Lebanon is trying to undermine terrorist recruitment by enacting better health care and education reform. Which programs do you think will be the most effective at neutralizing the call to extremism?

3. After reading the viewpoints in this chapter—and perhaps investigating how other Arab governments are handling terrorism—explain whether you think Middle Eastern regimes are committed to fighting extremism within their borders. List the reasons why these governments might want to support the war on terror and the reasons they might not wish to be so committed to it.

Organizations to Contact

The editors have compiled the following list of organizations concerned with the issues debated in this book. The descriptions are derived from materials provided by the organizations. All have publications or information available for interested readers. The list was compiled on the date of publication of the present volume; the information provided here may change. Be aware that many organizations take several weeks or longer to respond to inquiries, so allow as much time as possible.

American Enterprise Institute (AEI)
1150 Seventeenth Street NW, Washington, DC   20036
(202) 862-5800 • fax: (202) 862-7177
Web site: www.aei.org

American Enterprise Institute (AEI) is a conservative organization that promotes the ideas of limited government, private enterprise, individual liberty, and vigilant national defense and foreign policies. The institute employs its fellows and scholars to provide reports and commentary concerning current political issues in the United States. AEI believes that democratic reform in the Middle East is key to stabilizing the region; that the war in Iraq has created a new ally in the war on terrorism; and that Iran is a continuing threat to the United States. In addition, the institute strongly supports a close relationship between the United States and Israel. *The American* is the bimonthly magazine of AEI; articles from this publication as well as other reports and op-eds can be accessed from the AEI Web site.

American Israel Public Affairs Committee (AIPAC)
251 H Street NW, Washington, DC   20001
(202) 639-5200 • fax: (202) 347-4918
Web site: www. aipac.org

The American Israel Public Affairs Committee AIPAC is the pro-Israel lobby to the American government, which seeks to ensure Israel's security by promoting a strong pro-Israel U.S. foreign policy. Lobbyists for the organization seek support from both Democrats and Republicans in both the congressional and executive branches of government. AIPAC has worked to guarantee continued foreign aid to Israel and to extend support for stopping Iran's nuclear program. Organization publications and backgrounders on current issues regarding U.S. foreign policy toward Israel are available on the committee's Web site.

Brookings Institution
1775 Massachusetts Avenue NW, Washington, DC   20036
(202) 797-6000
e-mail: communications@brookings.edu
Web site: www.brookings.edu

Based in Washington, DC, the Brookings Institution is a research organization that conducts independent research in order to construct policy recommendations which it believes will make the American democracy stronger, guarantee that all Americans have social and economic security and opportunity, and ensure that the international system remains stable and open. Scholars at the institution have written extensively on the situation in the Middle East with articles on topics such as the American occupation in both Iraq and Afghanistan, democracy in the Middle East, and Arab-Israeli relations. These articles are all available via the Web site.

Carnegie Endowment for International Peace
1779 Massachusetts Avenue NW
Washington, DC   20036-2103
(202) 483-7600 • fax: (202) 483-1840
e-mail: info@carnegieendowment.org
Web site: www.carnegieendowment.org

Founded in 1910, the Carnegie Endowment for International Peace has been working for nearly 100 years to promote international cooperation between all nations and to encourage the

United States to take an active role on the world scene with the ultimate goal of advancing global peace and stability. With regard to the Middle East, the organization offers comprehensive research on a wide range of issues from the Arab-Israeli conflict to the war in Iraq, and from regional democratic reform to the importance of continuing engagement with Iran. Carnegie Endowment publishes the monthly *Arab Reform Bulletin*.

Cato Institute

1000 Massachusetts Avenue NW
Washington, DC   20001-5403
(202) 842-0200 • fax: (202) 842-3490
Web site: www.cato.org

The Cato Institute, a libertarian organization, seeks to advance the ideas of limited government intervention in both the social and economic lives of Americans, promotes a free market economic system, and rejects overzealous military intervention in foreign affairs. Scholars at the institute have been calling for a U.S. departure from Iraq since 2004 and favor a diplomatic relationship with Iran to ensure that its nuclear program remains for domestic use only. Cato has numerous publications such as the tri-annual *Cato Journal*, the quarterly *Cato's Letters*, and the quarterly *Regulation*.

Center for American Progress (CAP)

1333 H Street NW, 10th Floor, Washington, DC   20005
(202) 682-1611 • fax: (202) 682-1867
e-mail: progress@americanprogress.org
Web site: www.americanprogress.org

The Center for American Progress (CAP) seeks to promote a liberal and progressive agenda and believes that America should take its role as international leader to ensure peace and stability worldwide, especially in the Middle East. The organization advocates for a U.S. policy in the region that would withdraw troops from Iraq but continue involvement and dialogue between the two countries. Reports on current situations in the Middle East can be read on its Web site.

Center for Strategic and International Studies (CSIS)

1800 K Street NW, Washington, DC
(202) 887-0200 • fax: (202) 775-3199
Web site: www.csis.org

Experts at the Center for Strategic and International Studies (CSIS) research and analyze issues relating to defense and security policy, global problems, and regional studies in order to provide policy suggestions for individuals in government. The Middle East program at CSIS focuses on advancing increased understanding of the region and analyzing the forces at work in shaping the ongoing conditions there. Analysis focuses on individual countries as well as the impact of the petroleum industry and the global dependence on this region for its energy supply. The *Washington Quarterly* is the official publication of CSIS.

Council on Foreign Relations (CFR)

The Harold Pratt House, 58 East Sixty-Eighth Street
New York, NY   10065
(212) 434-9400 • fax: (212) 434-9800
Web site: www.cfr.org

The Council on Foreign Relations (CFR) is a nonpartisan, membership organization seeking to provide information and insight on current foreign policy issues in America. The council seeks to further understanding of foreign policy concerns by sponsoring meetings for global leaders to debate the current issues and operates a think tank where scholars from a variety of backgrounds can provide current commentary on foreign policy. While CFR does not take any official position on these issues, it does provide extensive background reports on topics such as the war in Iraq, Iran, and the Israeli-Palestinian conflict. *Foreign Affairs* is the bi-monthly magazine published by the council.

Heritage Foundation

214 Massachusetts Avenue NE, Washington, DC   20002-4999
(202) 546-4400

e-mail: info@heritage.org
Web site: www.heritage.org

The Heritage Foundation is a conservative think tank dedicated to preserving the principles of limited government, free market economics, and a strong national defense in America. Foundation experts publish reports on all topics ranging from economics, to foreign policy, to education. With regard to the current situation in the Middle East, the Heritage Foundation states, it "has become perhaps the most crucial regional arena for American foreign policy in the coming years." Additionally, the organization sees the Hamas-led Palestinian government as a major barrier to the brokering of a peace agreement between Palestine and Israel, believes a democratic Iraq is an important ally in the war against terrorism, and warns that Iran is a threat to the United States and its allies. Reports and commentary on these and other topics can be read on the Heritage Web site.

Hoover Institution on War, Revolution, and Peace

434 Galvez Mall, Stanford University
Stanford, CA 94305-6010
(650) 723-1754 • fax: (650) 723-1687
Web site: www.hoover.org

The Hoover Institution on War, Revolution and Peace focuses its work on the in-depth analysis of politics, economics, domestic and foreign political economies, and international affairs. Scholars at the organization seek to further the debate on current issues in the United States and the global community by providing pertinent research and commentary on a wide variety of topics. The Hoover Institution also sponsors programs that seek to further explore these issues, such as the Iran Democracy Project, which was established to develop a better understanding of the possibilities for advancing democracy in Iran and the rest of the Middle East. Reports on other topics relating to Middle East issues can be viewed on the organization's Web site in addition to previous issues of the Hoover Institution's bimonthly publication *Policy Review* or the quarterly *Hoover Digest*.

Middle East Forum (MEF)

1500 Walnut Street, Suite 1050, Philadelphia, PA 19102
(215) 546-5406 • fax: (215) 546-5409
e-mail: info@meforum.org
Web site: www.meforum.org

The think tank, Middle East Forum (MEF), works to define America's role in the Middle East, a region it sees as a continuing problem for the United States and its allies. The forum promotes a U.S. foreign policy in the region that fights radical Islam, implores Palestinians to accept Israel, works to improve democratic reform, and counters the threat from Iran. MEF's official publication, *Middle East Quarterly*, provides research and articles from the forum's scholars on contemporary issues in the Middle East; additional articles can be read on the organization's Web site.

Middle East Policy Council (MEPC)

1730 M Street NW, Suite 512, Washington, DC 20036
e-mail: info@mepc.org
Web site: www.mepc.org

Founded in 1981, the Middle East Policy Council (MEPC) provides political analysis of issues relating specifically to the Middle East and encourages ongoing debate and education by sponsoring conferences for educators and government officials. Articles assessing U.S. involvement in the region, the Arab-Israeli conflict, and the ongoing situation in Iran can be accessed on the MEPC Web site. The quarterly journal *Middle East Policy* is the organization's official publication.

Project on Middle East Democracy (POMED)

PO Box 25533, Washington, DC 20027-8533
(202) 422-6804
Web site: www.pomed.org

Project on Middle East Democracy (POMED) was founded with the goal of analyzing the ways in which democratic reform in the Middle East could benefit the region and its people, and to assess the best strategies for the United States to pursue in order to support this reform. The organization seeks to further its aims through dialogue, research, and advocacy. POMED, however, is critical of the current methods of democratic reform in the region, and insists that "military-led regime change" is not a productive way of promoting democracy. Articles and reports by POMED scholars can be accessed on its Web site.

Washington Institute for Near East Policy
1828 L Street NW, Suite 1050, Washington, DC   20036
(202) 452-0650 • fax: (202) 223-5364
Web site: www.washingtoninstitute.org

The Washington Institute for Near East Policy seeks to increase understanding of the relationship between the United States and the Middle East as a region. Additionally, the organization insists that peace and stability will only be ensured if the two remain actively engaged. Research areas focus on individual countries in the region as well as on larger issues such as the peace process, proliferation, terrorism, and U.S. policy. Reports on these issues and others can all be read online.

Bibliography of Books

Arshin Adib-Moghaddam *Iran in World Politics: The Question of the Islamic Republic.* New York: Columbia University Press, 2008.

Fakhreddin Azim *The Quest for Democracy in Iran: A Century of Struggle Against Authoritarian Rule.* Cambridge, MA: Harvard University Press, 2008.

Gawdat Bahgat *Proliferation of Nuclear Weapons in the Middle East.* Gainesville, FL: University Press of Florida, 2007.

David Barsamian *Targeting Iran.* San Francisco, CA: City Lights, 2007.

Benazir Bhutto *Reconciliation: Islam, Democracy, and the West.* New York: Harper, 2008.

Jason Brownlee *Authoritarianism in an Age of Democratization.* New York: Cambridge University Press, 2007.

Daniel Byman *The Five Front War: The Better Way to Fight Global Jihad.* Hoboken, NJ: John Wiley & Sons, 2008.

Jack Caravelli *Nuclear Insecurity: Understanding the Threat from Rogue Nations and Terrorists.* Westport, CT: Praeger Security International, 2008.

Thomas Carothers & Marina Ottaway, eds.

Uncharted Journey: Promoting Democracy in the Middle East. Washington, DC: Carnegie Endowment for International Peace, 2005.

Noam Chomsky

Failed States: The Abuse of Power and the Assault on Democracy. New York: Metropolitan, 2006.

Larry Jay Diamond

The Spirit of Democracy: The Struggle to Build Free Societies Throughout the World. New York: Times, 2008.

Gwynne Dyer

After Iraq: Anarchy and Renewal in the Middle East. New York: Thomas Dunne, 2008.

Charles Ferguson

No End in Sight: Iraq's Descent into Chaos. New York: PublicAffairs, 2008.

Nathan Gonzalez

Engaging Iran: The Rise of a Middle East Powerhouse and America's Strategic Choice. Westport, CT: Praeger Security International, 2007.

Robert W. Hefner, ed.

Remaking Muslim Politics: Pluralism, Contestation, Democratization. Princeton, NJ: Princeton University Press, 2005.

Roger Howard

Iran Oil: The New Middle East Challenge to America. New York: I.B. Tauris, 2007.

Russ Hoyle

Going to War: How Misinformation, Disinformation, and Arrogance Led America into Iraq. New York: Thomas Dunne, 2008.

Alireza Jafarzadeh *The Iran Threat: President Ahmadinejad and the Coming Nuclear Crisis.* New York: Palgrave, 2007.

Rashid Khalidi *Resurrecting Empire: Western Footprints and America's Perilous Path in the Middle East.* Boston: Beacon, 2004.

Michael A. Ledeen *The Iranian Time Bomb: The Mullah Zealots' Quest for Destruction.* New York: Truman Talley, 2007.

Saree Makdisi *Palestine Inside Out: An Everyday Occupation.* New York: W.W. Norton, 2008.

John J. Mearsheimer & Stephen M. Walt *The Israel Lobby and U.S. Foreign Policy.* New York: Farrar, Straus and Giroux, 2007.

Aaron David Miller *The Much Too Promised Land: America's Elusive Search for Arab-Israeli Peace.* New York: Bantam, 2008.

Ziba Mir-Hosseini & Richard Tapper, eds. *Islam and Democracy in Iran: Eshkevari and the Quest for Reform.* New York: I.B. Tauris, 2006.

Kevin P. Phillips *American Theocracy: The Peril and Politics of Radical Religion, Oil, and Borrowed Money in the 21st Century.* New York: Viking 2006.

Marsha Pripstein Posusney & Michele Penner Angrist *Authoritarianism in the Middle East: Regimes and Resistance.* Boulder, CO: Lynne Rienner, 2005.

Barry Rubin   *The Long War for Freedom: The Arab Struggle for Democracy in the Middle East.* Hoboken, NJ: John Wiley & Sons, 2006.

Donald M. Snow   *What After Iraq?* New York: Pearson/Longman, 2009.

David S. Sorenson   *An Introduction to the Modern Middle East: History, Religion, Political Economy, Politics.* Boulder, CO: Westview, 2008.

Robin Wright   *Dreams and Shadows: The Future of the Middle East.* New York: Penguin, 2008.

Index